THE COMING
RACE WARS?

ALSO BY WILLIAM PANNELL . . .

Evangelism From the Bottom Up

THE COMING
RACE WARS?

A *Cry* for Reconciliation

William Pannell

*Forewords by John M. Perkins
and Jay Kesler*

ZondervanPublishingHouse
Academic and Professional Books
Grand Rapids, Michigan

A Division of HarperCollins*Publishers*

Requests for information should be addressed to:
Zondervan Publishing House
Academic and Professional Books
Grand Rapids, Michigan 49530

Edited by Randy Frame and James E. Ruark
Interior design by James E. Ruark
Cover design by John Lucas
Cover photo by Mike Carter Photography

Library of Congress Cataloging-in-Publication Data
Pannell, William E.
    The coming race wars? : a cry for reconciliation / William E. Pannell.
        p.   cm.
    Includes bibliographical references.
    ISBN 0-310-38181-9
    1. United States—Race relations. 2. Racism—United States. 3. United States—Politics and government—1989– I. Title.
E184.A1P3   1993   92-41877
305.8′00973—dc20   CIP

Printed in the United States of America

93 94 95 96 97 98 / ML / 10 9 8 7 6 5 4 3 2 1

Contents

Foreword

John M. Perkins
President, John M. Perkins Foundation
for Reconciliation and Development

The continued deterioration of our urban communities and the recent injustice, violence, and destruction surrounding the Rodney King incident have given us a glimpse of what the future is going to be, unless the church grabs hold of its prime directive: to be God's reconciling agent in the world.

The central message of the gospel—demonstrated not only in Jesus' death, burial, and resurrection, but by the life that he lived—is to reconcile humanity to a holy God and to each other across racial, cultural, social, and economic barriers. By our love for one another will humanity know that we are Christians.

Bill Pannell's book is a timely, chilling indictment of a church that has failed to show that love in the area of race. Bill gives a powerful analysis of how so many of our churches today have fled the inner cities and removed themselves from the urban problem. As a result, many Christians find it very difficult to relate to the new urban dwellers, whether Black, Latino, Asian, or other ethnic groups.

I have known Bill for more than twenty years. *The Coming Race Wars? A Cry for Reconciliation* is a story based on his own experiences at the front lines of urban ministry as a youth worker with Youth for Christ, as a pastor, as an evangelist, and finally as a seminary professor.

Bill's book confronts the body of Christ today, just as John the Baptist confronted the people of his day when he said, "The axe is already at the root of the trees, and every tree that does not produce good fruit will be cut down and thrown into the fire." It is my prayer that this book will help inspire the people of God to rise up and take responsibility for offering a new reality within our nation—a witness of racial reconciliation that only we who claim the name of Jesus can provide.

Foreword

Jay Kesler
President, Taylor University

Most of us have seen at least one film, if not several, in which the storytelling device is a black man and a white man shackled together attempting to escape from prison. The vehicle has been adapted to man and child, man and woman, cowboy and Indian, father and son, man and dog, woman and alien, and across the whole spectrum of possible human relationships. The theme insists that each can learn to understand the other, both can be right or wrong at various times, and each lacks the ability to understand the other without sustained contact in real-life situations. (Such is the case of black and white in America—such is the case with Bill Pannell and me.) Bill and I have been bound together for all our adult lives by the unbreakable bond of the Gospel of Christ and our personal commitment to Christian love and family friendship.

This book is a book filled with rage, innuendo, stereotype, grace, research, blindness, gentleness, insight, bias, despair, evenhandedness, and hope; in short, the full range of human emotions. Bill Pannell is a faithful friend of the Gospel and a friend of mine, but it does hurt. I am fully aware that I am an "evangelical leader," not totally by earned distinction, but sometimes more like Peter Sellers, by just "being there." I, like other white males of European extraction and believers in Jesus Christ, am guilty of not making the institutions I serve and influence more responsive to the needs of the disenfranchised, the poor among us, various minorities, and African-Americans in particular. As leaders we feel important, confused, lacking in resources, and misunderstood. Most who actually have power would give it up immediately to escape the responsibilities involved. Those without power feel if they had it, they could do better. This book pushes us to try to do better.

Bill sees malice of forethought, lack of resolve, hunger for power, insular thinking, and racism in many of our institutions, activities, and leadership. On the other side, I meet very few— certainly not as many as in the sixties—white evangelical leaders who hold racist views or who countenance such positions in others unless, of course, you define racism as being endemic in the white race and therefore to claim to be otherwise is hypocrisy. I do not mind working under that definition if all others admit that they are also racist based on the fact of their pigmentation.

This attitude is certainly not the position Pannell takes in his book. Bill fears the balkanization of the earth's peoples over race, gender, religion, class, or ethnicity and clings to the Christian ideal of peace and unity. He will not allow this vision of harmony, however, to be gained at the expense of biblical justice. This is why he insists on bringing us back to the issues of systemic injustice, racism, and political expediency. He cries out for the ideals of Martin Luther King lest in despair and unrelenting frustration youth choose the model of Minister Farrakhan.

I could wish that Bill had placed more stress on personal holiness and biblical personal ethics. He is aware that others will make this observation. However, he argues that in addition to personal salvation we acknowledge the need to address social injustices in the name of Christ. He wants us to see that even though the ground has shifted since the sixties, the underlying conditions remain unchanged or have deteriorated. It is worse to be male and black in America now than in the fifties and sixties in terms of employment and dignity based on opportunity. He understands the "white backlash" against affirmative action, yet aches because the injustices persist and continue to grow.

I believe every caring white Christian will profit from reading this book through to the end. Many will disagree with its conclusions; however, none will doubt the visceral truthfulness of the message. Bill is telling it like he sees it to be and too often as it actually is. He is frustrated with the lack of progress. He largely agrees with white conservatives that the old liberalism has failed to bring solutions. He is angry, however, that we have not responded as a church to work for solutions. He resents our too-often-expressed glee over the failure of liberalism and our failure to see the insensitivity and callousness of our conservatism.

"I think you owe it to me as my friend to fight me, to let me get away with nothing, to force me to be honest, to allow me to take no refuge in rage or in despair . . . and of course, I owe you the same. This means we are certainly going to hurt each other's feelings from time to time. But that's one of the ways in which people learn from each other." These words from James Baldwin quoted by Bill Pannell aptly describe the contents of this book as it impacts me.

I thank Bill for his insistence on bringing up unsolved agendas, even when I am weary of hearing them again. They must be our agendas together in the name of biblical justice. Frankly, I thought we were doing a little better—I thought Bill did also—yet in the immediate aftermath of the Los Angeles riots and the obvious fragility of the racial atmosphere, especially among the young, this book encourages us to take a deep breath and commit ourselves once again to the task of understanding, justice, and evangelism together. We are, after all, "one in the bonds of love," and that love was not only painful but costly in the ultimate sense.

Others in our culture may have become weary of the struggle for understanding and become willing to hide in the enclaves of their ethnicity and multiculturalism. However, this option is not available to Christians. We must continue to confront in love and to listen to each other and seek the unity that consumed Jesus in his high priestly prayer in John 17.

Very few people, black or white today, seem to possess the

courage to speak truthfully of their true feelings across the racial divide. Bill is taking the risk one more time, and I am proud to be trusted with his fear of rejection. He hurts, I hurt, we hurt together; however, we have not yet "resisted unto death, striving against sin." Bill is not, by nature, a combative person. He is open, friendly, and conciliatory; he is also honest about his views and open to challenge. It is my sincere prayer that the considerable good will and personal relationships that have developed between black and white Christians over the last two decades will unite us in a concerted new effort together to bring the power of Christ to bear on the issues of social injustice, family values, personal holiness, and eternal salvation. We agree together that the church is the best possible hope in a fallen world.

Introduction

Moneta J. Sleet, Jr., is a photojournalist, and a good one. He won the Pulitzer Prize in 1969, the first black person—and practitioner of that art who worked exclusively for black publications—to receive that award. His work has been displayed in major exhibitions from the Metropolitan Museum of Art in New York City to the City Art Museum in St. Louis to the Detroit Public Library. He has also won the prestigious citation for excellence from the Overseas Press Club of America.

Mr. Sleet attracted my attention while I was reading a review of some of his work and his explanation for his success. The reasons he advances for that success are far-reaching, ranging from the mastery of the technical demands of photography to much patience and sensitivity to his subject matter. But he offers the following as the major reason:

> I must say that I wasn't there as an objective reporter. To be perfectly honest I had something to say, or at least I hoped that I did, and was trying to show one side of it—because we didn't have any trouble finding the other side. So I was intentionally emotionally involved. That may not be good school of journalism, but that's the way I felt (C. Gerald Fraser, "The Vision of Moneta Sleet," *New York Times*, 19 October 1986).

This book will not win a Pulitzer Prize. It will probably not even impress the Evangelical Press Association. But this much I hope for—that readers will hear my views, attempt to feel what I feel, and respect my choice to abandon claims to objectivity. Like Mr. Sleet, I have something to say, or at least I hope I do. I admit I am telling one side of the story, as I have witnessed it. The other side is well-known, at least by African-Americans. That other side controls the media, especially the so-called Christian media. It creates the definitions and lays out the boundaries and guidelines that determine the discourse, including Christian discourse.

I was not very well acquainted with the rules of the game the other side plays until I wrote a book, published in 1968, called *My Friend, the Enemy* (Waco, Tex.: Word Books). As the title suggests, I set out to explain how white people, including people I knew and loved well, could at once be both friend and foe. I attempted to tell what it was like, from my point of view, to be evangelical and black among countrymen and Christians whose captivity to the ideology of white supremacy was scarcely admitted and seldom challenged from within its ranks. I had hoped the book would open doors for discourse and reconciliation.

It did and it didn't.

Those who responded most favorably were often found in more liberal theological circles, including the more liberal among evangelicals. In the evangelical camp, "liberal" should be understood not so much in theological terms as in the sense of the marriage of theology and social action—orthodoxy to orthopraxis. Some of these liberal evangelicals, to their credit, were working on that marriage, which was not always the case among theological liberals. For others, mainly those in more conservative evangelical circles, my book proved to be a bit intimidating. To be sure, I received a number of invitations to speak during the years following the book's release. (It came to be unthinkable in these circles to hold a major convocation without one of us.) But long after all the coffee was drunk and the little sandwiches eaten, the uneasy smiles were retracted and it became clear that reconciliation with most of these saints was still a ways off. In fact, it was a long ways off.

Now, in the shadow of a new century, more than twenty

years after my first attempt to reflect openly on this experience from the other side, I have decided to revisit My Friend. We are both older and perhaps wiser, maybe even more "Christian." We are certainly more cautious and, all things considered, we are both more conservative. We all have two cars and hold property by now, and many of us have been grandparents for some time. My sons have grown up and have become professional people. My oldest married "one of them," a marvelous human being possessed of an impeccable Presbyterian heritage that stretches from La Canada to Korea and back. Have mercy!

I have settled down somewhat in a faculty position at a prestigious evangelical seminary, having left the more harried confines of Detroit from which I viewed the world in 1968. I am no longer running through airports trying to catch up with Tom Skinner on the way to another evangelistic crusade. L.B.J. is dead, as are a number of other Democrats still walking about in the land. Richard Nixon is alive, of course, experiencing another of his reincarnations, advising presidents about foreign policy from his hideout in New York City. The country, My Friend included, seems to have slipped happily into the dream world of conservative (or neo-conservative, if you will) politics, drunk on the heavy elixirs dispensed by an aged Republican from California's horse country. We will be living with Reagan long after he's gone.

This book, once more, is about My Friend: *Rabbit Redux* without the style. It is an attempt to answer the question put to me with increasing frequency, "If you were to write that book today, how would you write it? Have we made any progress?" I suspect that the question is raised because in the past several years overt racism has again reared its head among us—on college campuses, in quiet neighborhoods far removed from center cities, and among judges and other elected officials. It powerfully affects discussions of what is officially labeled "multiculturalism" at major universities and seminaries. It allows a fresh-faced, former Klansman to enjoy considerable success in contending for high public office.

The question is also raised, I suspect, because Christians, like most Americans these days, are possessed of a strong sense of nationalism. Thus they need to believe the country has made great strides in human relations. Surely we are more humane than Arabs or even Jews; than white South Africans; than Muslims in Afghanistan. We want to know we are better than we were in the sixties. It is important to our sense of nationhood that we believe we have made progress based on our cherished democratic ideals, despite the fact that most of the news about black people, written at times by us, has not been good. Twelve years of presidents Reagan and Bush have only served to confuse the issue, making us wonder how much progress we really have made.

Then, too, it seems there has been a long-standing psychological need among white Americans—Englishmen, too, I suspect—to be somehow validated by colored people. This need is related to occasional fits of guilt from all those centuries of oppression aimed at people of color worldwide. White people may still feel the need for black approbation in order to be freed from this guilt. This feeling may be the flip side of what historian George M. Fredrickson called "romantic racialism," according to which black people are gentle savages in need of domestication in the big house of democracy. This is akin to a Western view of the untamed animals of Africa. It is hard to imagine a world without them. They seem to fit into our Western need to see all things as existing for our benefit and comfort. Without them, we would have had to invent a Hemingway.

Be that as it may, I found myself indoors one night last spring, my evening reverie having been dispelled amid the swirl of events assaulting my senses as I watched the city of Los Angeles via television. I listened to a local newsman commenting on a conversation between distraught citizens in Long Beach who were disagreeing vehemently about the causes of the riots. In his wrap-up, the commentator referred to the one man as "Afro-American" and to the white man as "the gentleman on the left of your screen." The world had been divided between gentlemen and Africans; we and they; them and us; white and black. What struck me most was that the white man had no clue as to what the black man to whom he was listening was trying to say, even after the black man produced a card signifying his full-time Vietnam tenure. My African-American brother was trying to say that rioting is not about groceries or stolen TVs. It is about being a black man in white America. It is about the conviction—the awful, choking, suffocating conviction—that a black man has no value that a white legal system can be counted upon to uphold.

This book is occasioned also because Christians experience some paroxysms of curiosity about their theology of reconciliation. After all the turmoil of the past twenty-five years at home and abroad, and after all the noise about evangelism and growing churches, there is still the sense that reconciliation represents the unfinished agenda of the church. Uneasiness about this is stimulated by the realization that the American scene is no longer a simple matter of black and white. The culture is pluralistic beyond the average American's understanding. Even after years of hearing about homogeneous, racial-ethnic units for purposes of everything from real estate to church growth, the notion that reconciliation is still a Christian ideal simply won't go away.

For white American Christians, this issue, at gut level and historically, is still primarily an issue between African-Americans and Euro-Americans. The other folks among us are still "foreigners." Black people and white people, whatever else they might be, are Americans. So this is a "family" issue, a homegrown feud. I have heard the question phrased like this: "Can we really make this pilgrim journey together and, if so, at what price, if it is to be made with integrity?" I am reminded of a conversation between two of this country's finest writers. The exchange took place in the pages of a magazine shortly after the fires of Watts had inflamed the emotions of a nation in 1965. The late James Baldwin was spelling out the price of brotherhood to Budd Shulberg. The esteem they held for one another was evident. It was Baldwin's contention that the price of brotherhood was confrontation:

> I think you owe it to me, as my friend, to fight me, to let me get away with nothing, to force me to be clear, to force me to be honest, to allow me to take no refuge in rage or in despair . . . and of course, I owe you the same. This means that we are certainly going to hurt each other's feelings from time to time. But that's one of the ways in which people learn from each other.

I am quite sure the book I have written has shortcomings, more of them than I know. But I am aware of this one: My Friend, who is still the enemy, has no voice in these pages. My argument is one-sided in the extreme; it is a monologue. I acknowledge here—and now and again throughout the book— that the issues and problems are sometimes not as simple as I make them seem. But I believe it is important for me—and for My Friend—that I say what I have to say, even if at times it smacks of bitterness and sounds unreasonable. If my words are unguarded, they are at least sincere.

If there is any justification for such an approach, it is that I couldn't believe that My Friend was even interested in the subject any longer. I have had to struggle to believe that he does not consider me—and those I symbolize—redundant. I am quite sure My Friend has nothing against me personally, especially to the extent that many of my values, norms, and theological constructs are one and the same with his. But when I insist on being black, as I did twenty years ago, I find myself once again a nonperson.

In 1968 it was possible to write a book as if My Friend were male and as if the people I represented were also male. As I re-read that earlier work, I am a bit embarrassed at the male-oriented language and viewpoint. I could perhaps be excused then, but not now. I know that being a black male does not automatically make one nonsexist in attitude or behavior. To be so calls for as radical a conversion for black males as I would call for among white people with regard to their attitudes toward colored peoples.

Yet it seems clear that the crisis in black communities today is the crisis of the black male. Every conceivable way must be found to restore this endangered species to a place in the human family. So this book, at bottom, is about the black male in a white society, the black male in a pluralistic society wherein the newest Americans have no idea what the black race has been through historically and have very little time to invest in understanding how that history has affected black men. There is money to be made here in America. Therefore understanding—and the justice that accompanies it—can wait.

Yet, surely, black men will not make it without black women, even though the relationships between the genders often border on open conflict. It is tough enough to be a woman in a man's world, but to be a black woman in a world where black men are marginal or even nonexistent in any wholesome sense must be excruciating. The dynamics of these relationships by and large constitute uncharted territory in the history of African peoples on these shores. I will make little attempt to deal with this matter here: it falls outside the purview of this book. I am not qualified to deal with it anyway. But the church had better deal with it soon if it is to have any relevance to the black family and to the traditional understanding of Christian marriage.

I have not attempted in this book to seek out many sources outside my experience. Those I have confronted are identified in the text. You will not find most of them at your neighborhood Christian bookstore, which is another piece of the problem. In any case, this book is not a bibliography. Rather, it is an attempt to lay my thoughts alongside those of many others.

This will very likely be my final visit with My Friend, on paper at least. I have tried to contact him before through the pages of leading Christian journals. But they would not print my thoughts the way I wanted to express them—that would be bad for profits. So I am grateful to this publisher, whose representatives assured me they would print what I wanted to say the way I wanted to say it. So if it comes off badly, I take the blame. At least I will have gotten something off my chest.

But there is another reason I may not write another book. I fear we may be headed into an America with little time to read. We are on the very brink of a police state wherein law and order will mean something far more aggressive than it did when Richard Nixon inhabited the White House. If there is another urban uprising, it will not be a riot, but a war—one that could trigger W. E. B. DuBois's dark prophecy that the century would end in a devastating race war. Such a conflict has been simmering ever since the first boatload of slaves debarked on these shores. I hope we have come too far for something this disastrous to take place. But just in case, if we are going to get together, we had best do it quickly.

Chapter One

Here We Go Again

Negroes firmly believe that police brutality and harassment occur repeatedly in Negro neighborhoods. This belief is unquestionably one of the major reasons for intense Negro resentment against the police (U.S. Riot Commission Report, March 1968).

When I was a kid I got hit in the head by accident with a ball bat. My vision blurred, my ears vibrated with a sound like a distant bell, and my legs turned to Silly Putty. I felt the impact clear down to my stomach. And what was worse, after my head began to clear, was the embarrassment that this should happen to me. I was too alert, too athletic, to be the victim of such a thing. Maybe it could happen to one of my sisters, but not to me.

A riot is like getting hit in the head with a ball bat. No one sees it coming, and when struck we reel like emotional drunkards for weeks afterward. We grope for balance; we are betrayed by behaviors that are embarrassing to recall six weeks later. In the aftermath of the Los Angeles violence of 1992, people of all races confessed together that we had never smiled at so many Hispanics in our lives; nor noticed with deference so many black people; nor felt so uneasy around Koreans.

I remember exactly where I was when the rumble started. I was sitting in my car, feet resting on the driveway pavement. It is a nice set of wheels, new and red. It is evening, a time to watch the sun romance the nearby mountains, receiving in return a blush of soft crimson. This night, though, the sky is gray and the sun has surrendered to the times. There is a soft whiff of smoke in the air. I know what it is and whence it comes. And I wish I could turn more than my back against it. But one of the burdens of being a black male is that smoke follows you. This time it is Los Angeles. Twenty-seven years after the riots in Watts, the City of Deferred Dreams explodes like a raisin in the sun. Again.

In 1965 I was in Detroit. I confess to a certain smugness then. We "knew" it would not happen to us. It did, of course. In 1992 in my cozy neighborhood, now eerily quiet, I experience *déjà vu*. Old images rush to mind, and what's worse, old emotions: remorse, regret, fear, anger—especially anger. Justified or not, I am forced to admit that I don't like cops—not black cops, not Hispanic cops, not white cops. They are not the Constables on Patrol they used to be; they haven't been for years. Instead, unfortunately, I have come to view them more as an army of occupation, with citizens playing the role of civilians. And hard as I try to overcome my bias, I must admit that I especially don't like white cops. Not only do they preoccupy my mind, but they are in my guts. The taste is like bile.

The L.A. riots were triggered by an encounter between white cops and a black man. That's nothing new. Robert Conot, historian of riots in Los Angeles, observes that the Watts uprising began when a California Highway patrolman followed a black male off the freeway and attempted an arrest. Twenty-seven years later, a California Highway patrolman followed a black man and his companions and called for local backup, and the rest is history. Rodney King became part of black urban lore. Black people will recall his name, as they recall the name of Emmett Till. True, Rodney King's personal life to date leaves much to be desired. He might admit to that himself. True, he violated the law and should have been arrested. Still, he is a human being, created in the image of God, deserving of dignity even in his sinfulness. But to out-of-control cops that night, he was just another gorilla in the mist.

Yet the revelation of Rodney King's brutal beating at the hands of four white cops was not what triggered a riot. After all, this was merely another in a lifetime of incidents black men have suffered at the hands of police. Not all of them have been captured on video. What set off the riots was the decision of a predominantly white jury to acquit the four officers. The policemen were tried by a jury of their peers, and their white peers found them guiltless. From all appearances, the white system had worked for white police officers.

The decision shocked the entire nation, black and white alike. For millions of white Americans, the decision starkly revealed that racism is not nearly so dead as they thought it was. Many white people were as puzzled and outraged as black people. Yet, for the most part, whites are in the position to maintain some emotional distance from the decision and its implications. For the most part, they did not take to the streets, burn down the town, or loot stores. We can hope that many wrote their congressmen, called mayors' offices across the country, or sent telegrams to President Bush. More importantly, we can hope that white people, especially Christians, understood more of the feelings of desperation and helplessness so prevalent among their black brothers and sisters.

By and large, black people, unlike whites, could not help but take this decision more personally. They had seen this script before. It was not the first time black people in Los Angeles had suffered severe reprimands to their humanity at the hands of white representatives of the legal system. Just months before the King incident, Latasha Harlins, age twelve, was murdered in a neighborhood store. The killer was a Korean shopkeeper, angered by what appeared to her to be the girl's attempt to steal an item from the store. What was recorded on the store's television surveillance system revealed the cold-blooded killing of the young girl as she was walking toward the front door. After a long and sensational trial, Soon Ja Du was found guilty of voluntary manslaughter. A white judge sentenced her to a ten-year suspended prison term, with five years of probation, four hundred hours of community service, and a five-hundred-dollar fine.

During this same period, two black men were released from prison after serving seventeen years. New evidence conclusively demonstrated they had been telling the truth all along, that they were innocent of the crime of which they had been charged and convicted. The evidence also indicated that the men had been "set up" by local police.

Then there was Eula Love, a black woman trying to find her way through the maze of gas-telephone-utility-company regulations and frustrated because service had been shut off. By the time the police arrived to settle an increasingly volatile relationship between her and the company, she had armed herself with a knife. Cornered in her backyard, she pulled that knife and was promptly shot several times. It was Eula with a knife against four cops armed with plenty of bullets, but not with know-how or training to subdue a lone woman nor with the patience to reason with her. Maybe they were busy that day, and it saved time just to "blow her away."

This is part of the context within which blacks viewed the not-guilty verdict in the Rodney King case. There is more.

Black people remember, for example, the spectacle of the Iran-Contra scandal: hundreds of hours of prime-time exposure on television, the expenditure of millions of tax dollars. What was the result of all that sound and fury? One new Marine Corps hero who spent some country-club prison time, then emerged to write a book and make speeches at Liberty University.

Then there were the savings and loan scandals: Michael Milken, Ivan Boesky, Wall Street, and international and multi-national banking scams implicating some of the top names in American politics and business. Black people know that most of those people will escape serious damage and will live to cheat again from deep in their suburban hideaways. But let a black man get followed off a freeway at night, and the brother's gone. The message this sends to black people is that if you are going to be a successful thief, you have to steal something really big— like the country. Or you could pull it off if your father happens to live in the White House.

Los Angeles is not in a class by itself. The litany of

mistreatment of blacks by our judicial and political systems could be easily recited in other cities. But again, these incidents by themselves do not explain the violent reaction either in Watts in 1965 or in greater Los Angeles in 1992. The real issues lie deeper today, as they did twenty-seven years ago. The 1968 Riot Commission Report, in its assessment of the causes of the Watts riots, said that

> disorder did not erupt as a result of a single "triggering" or "precipitating" incident. Instead, it was generated out of an increasingly disturbed social atmosphere, in which typically a series of tension-heightening incidents over a period of weeks or months became linked in the minds of many in the Negro community with a reservoir of underlying grievances (p. 6).

And what were these "underlying grievances"? According to the commission's research, they concerned "police practices, unemployment and underemployment, inadequate housing, inadequate education, poor recreation facilities and programs, and ineffectiveness of the political structure and grievance mechanisms." Other grievances cited included "disrespectful white attitudes, discriminatory administration of justice, inadequacy of federal programs, inadequacy of municipal services, discriminatory consumer and credit practices, and inadequate welfare programs" (p. 8).

Any list of grievances leading up to the riots of 1992 will contain most of those same items and maybe a few more.*

These are complex issues, wherein it is not always easy to assess human responsibility and pinpoint blame. Not everyone believes these ubiquitous concerns are capable of producing civil unrest to the point of outbreaks of destruction and violence. People of that ilk attribute the violence to the work of hoodlums, and, as the attorney general of the United States said, such behavior is not to be tolerated in a "civilized country." One local television personality, a former speechwriter for several Republican presidents, claimed that the riots were the work of "rotten people." Bruce Herschensohn, a Republican candidate for the U.S. Senate, said at a press conference

---

*A front-page report on the causes of the Los Angeles riots is headlined "Riot's Causes Same as in 60's, State Panel Says" (*Los Angeles Times*, 2 October 1992).

that "the underlying cause for burning, looting, stealing, and murder is that some people are rotten. That's the underlying cause, and those criminals exhibited no conscience and no empathy for the victims. It isn't society. It isn't a race. It isn't a circled-off locality. It's the individual" (*Los Angeles Times*, 6 May 1992, A4).

According to this conservative Republican argument, any assessment of the violence that blames society is wrong-headed liberalism. Thus no amount of government help would suffice because, in Herschensohn's words, "there's nothing that government can do about human nature.'

A corollary to this argument can be heard from the winner of the 1992 Templeton Prize for Progress in Religion. The Reverend Kyung-Chik Han argues that the problem in Los Angeles is the absence of a "Christian force" strong enough to promote racial harmony. Says Han, "Why don't you send missionaries to black people right here in this country? It seems to me the only way to solve social problems in this country is through mission efforts among the black people and the new immigrants" (*Los Angeles Times*, 16 May 1992, B5). Han, who won the million-dollar prize for his work among refugees and the poor, deserves credit for founding one of the largest churches in Seoul, Korea, the 60,000-member Young Nak Presbyterian Church. But he does not realize how simplistic and superficial his analysis of the riots sounds to black people. It should be acknowledged that what was reported in the popular press may not have been what Mr. Han intended. I do not have a high view of reporters' capacity to understand and interpret the words of evangelical speakers. But assuming that the press fairly portrayed Han on this occasion, his remarks represent another case of blaming the victims. If so, he could benefit from studying American history.

Others hear Han's argument as reflecting the view that the church is the only thing that matters. This view has never tolerated an admission that people need more than the church, more than Jesus, to make it. Instead, all that matters is that churches grow. If they grow because of riots, praise the Lord for the riots. Of course, Han was not saying that, but to many the logic implied in his words leads to that conclusion. And partly because he seems to offer the poor in Korea more than words, black people view his "wisdom" on the L.A. crisis as racist chauvinism at best, emanating from Korea and too easily dismissed as "culture." In two hundred years of living with racism, black people know how it sounds, no matter from what direction it comes or how it is cloaked. The point is that the nostrums of neither Herschensohn nor Han surprise black people. This is the same conservative claptrap we heard in the late sixties. My Friend kept asking me, "Don't you think that all that those people need is Jesus?" and I would say, "Well, you need more than Jesus. Why do you think we need less than you do?" Not even Jesus said that he was all that people needed. He fed the hungry, provided medical care for the lame, the halt, and the blind, and chided the ultra-conservatives in the religious establishment for their slavish devotion to tradition even as they ignored the claims of mercy and justice upon their resources.

Let me state for the record that I really do believe that people—all people—need Jesus. There is no other way to salvation. In Jesus Christ, all the fullness of the Godhead dwells bodily, and believers are complete in Him. All people of all colors need only Jesus for salvation. But to make it in society, white Christians—and not a few Korean brothers and sisters in this neighborhood—realize they need a lot more than salvation. They may expect black people to be content with salvation in Christ. But that is not enough for the white Christians themselves. So they work hard at their jobs—sometimes both parents around the clock. They send their children to private schools or academies. They spend lots of money on their kids, ranging from good nutrition to cultural opportunities.

People desire more than salvation. That is why most white Christians have voted their pocketbooks throughout the last decade. Whether or not the political agenda has represented the best interests of the poor and the marginal in the society is a minor consideration for those who eat well and are generally well sheltered against the elements. Most people vote out of self-interest. It is not relevant to most voters that innocent children and their families are trying to eke out a living against tough odds in the city. They would rather see to it that their own children have good jobs and credit cards and that their driveway runneth over with all sorts of wheels. Even when they go to the mission field, their passports give them a better umbrella than The Hartford—namely, access to the embassy. They always have a place to go when prayer meetings fail to halt the impending insurrection.

Nor is it surprising to hear the question again, "But why do they burn their own stores and homes?" Well, *they* don't. Black people who own homes or have small businesses don't burn them. The fires are set by others: frustrated, desperate, and mindless young people whose images the nation watched on network television. They were mindless but not dumb. Even in the midst of their orgy they knew that many of the properties burned in their communities are owned by persons and corporations who do not have the best interest of those communities at heart.

There were some cases, no doubt, of black- and Korean-owned businesses being torched by their owners—or people acting in their behalf—for the insurance. Some of these would be people acting out of frustration—desperate, disenfranchised people who have been unable to establish any financial viability and who have grown tired of watching white merchants, Jewish merchants—all kinds of people—getting off the plane and making a living in their community. These "foreigners" usually give nothing back. Instead they send their children to college with money made off black people. A black friend of mine put it like this: "These people get off the ___ plane, get met by a thousand relatives, drive off in fine cars, and the next week open a store in my neighborhood. And when my kid goes into his ___ store, he has the nerve to stare at him as if he was goin' to rob the place. We're tired of that ___."

Some people will ask the question, "If Koreans and Jewish merchants and others can succeed, why can't black people succeed in the same proportions?" The question suggests a fundamental lack of appreciation for the burden of black Americans, resulting from injustices of the past and present. We are talking about a race of people whose great-grandparents were in chains and regarded as subhuman, whose grandparents were forbidden to learn to read, whose parents have been victims of discrimination in the workplace, in the marketplace, in the academic world, and in the public square. We are talking about latent feelings of inferiority that are easily revived by the realities of contemporary racism. The question "Why can't blacks make it?" wrongly presumes that we start climbing from the same elevation.

It is not only the historical legacy of racism with which blacks must contend. There is also the racism of the current age. Given the complicated social policy questions and people analyzing affirmative action from different perspectives, the average black person might have trouble articulating his or her suspicion that somehow things are still not right: Black people still are not treated as if they are as worthy as others to pursue life, liberty, and happiness. The case of Rodney King was uncomplicated—something all blacks could understand: A black man was beaten, unnecessarily, by four white cops. The not-guilty verdict from the Simi Valley courtroom sent the clear message to black people that, after all these years, they still could not be considered fully human. Whether or not that message excuses the riots that followed the verdict, it certainly does explain them.

In spite of the similarities of the two riots twenty-seven years apart, there are some radical differences. In 1992, forty-five people died in riot-related incidents, more than for any other riot in the twentieth century. The scope of the destruction was greater than all the riots of the late sixties combined: one billion dollars. Insurance companies estimated they would lay out millions of dollars in riot claims. Additional millions were added to the budgets of the city and the country to provide firemen and national guardsmen.

In 1992, the scope was also greater in terms of the players involved. In the sixties the issues were clearly drawn, and they were between black people and white people. White people had begun migrating deep into the suburbs, and we have not seen each other for years. But many white people were still in the city in the late sixties, in our neighborhoods and along the boulevards of business. This is no longer the case. Today, to the extent that race is a factor in urban centers, the players are more likely to be a glorious mixture of peoples. (The largest number of people arrested in Los Angeles was Mexican youths. Korean businesses were devastated. White youths eventually got into the act, and black people were conspicuous.) To be sure, white businesses are still active in the city, even though often franchised through black managers. The business of America is still business, but those who occupy turf in central cities have changed. Word has gotten out, and many nations have come to the barbecue. Los Angeles's recent uprising was a rainbow affair.

The potential for violence between ethnic groups has been building for years. Indeed, a check of most major periodicals in the country reveals that, from the mid-eighties on, they have registered concern about the gathering storm in race relations in America. From Washington to New York City, from Philadelphia to Los Angeles, there have been repeated skirmishes between African-Americans and Asian-Americans. The Reverend H. P. Rachel, pastor of Greater New Unity Baptist Church in Watts, put it like this in an interview in July 1987: "Koreans and other groups are taking everything we got, and America is sitting by and letting it happen. You have a powder keg" (*Wall Street Journal*, 31 July 1987, p. 36).

The social struggle between blacks and whites is still a major fact of urban reality. But it is no longer the only reality. Today the social, cultural, and economic struggles are multidimensional. There is a struggle for economic turf between Koreans and blacks. Korean-Americans themselves are caught in the middle between the expectations and values of an older generation and their own, more distinctively American set of values. There is frustration and tension as Hispanic people move into neighborhoods that in the sixties were reserved for black people. Hispanics in the U.S. now number 22.4 million, or 9 percent of the country's population. And they are steadily becoming the next significant political force in the city.

Another major difference between the urban scene today and in the sixties is that the gap between the "haves" and "have-nots" has grown much wider, not just between whites and blacks, but more importantly, between blacks and blacks. Some blacks have taken great economic, political, and social strides since the great days of the civil rights movement. But not many were able to follow. Today 36 million people live in poverty in this land. About 47 percent of these people live in the central parts of our cities, compared with 30 percent in 1968. Black poverty is a significant component of urban reality. Sixty percent of the country's black people who live in poverty live at the core of our major cities.

Blacks, of course, are not the only ones who are poor. Issues of race must be viewed alongside such issues as urban economic policies and discrimination based on class. In general, the future looks grim. The number of poor people who live in the city is on the rise, as is the number of single-parent families. Even though these people are better educated now, they hold fewer jobs than in the past (*U.S. News and World Report*, 18 May 1992, pp. 40–41). Add to this the fact that fully one-fifth of all children in America are poor and that 50 percent of these are black, and you have a major urban crisis that defies any attempt at a quick fix. Perhaps Kevin Phillips, better than any other columnist, has put his finger on the real difference between the riots of the sixties and those of the spring of '92:

> The racial disorder of the '60s was a revolution of rising expectations; blacks were in a hurry to get their share of a prosperous America with an expanding economy. Today, after twelve years of the Reagan and Bush administrations, with the rich getting richer and the middle class and the poor stagnating . . . these riots . . . are a revolution of diminishing expectations (*Los Angeles Times*, 10 May 1992, M1).

Black people, trapped in central cities and in the vice-grip of poverty, feel abandoned across a broad front. Even the black "middle class" has evacuated these centers as did their white counterparts before them. Thus many upwardly mobile black middle-class people are no longer an available resource. The tendency of this class to abandon the old neighborhood has caused many analysts, black and white, to argue that the problem of the inner cities is more a problem of black bourgeoisie than of white racism. This is worth considering. An ex-gang member may still respond to the plight of his old neighborhood when word of an impending threat reaches his ears in Beverly Hills. He simply straps on his piece, drops into his BMW, and heads for South Central.

This is not always the case with black upper-middle-class people or with the instant-millionaire sports celebrities. Not many people in the ghettoes view these stars as role models, no matter what ESPN or high-priced advertisers think of them.

When the smoke clears—especially the political smoke, which is the most oppressive smoke of all—it will become clearer that black political power has seriously eroded in the past decade. In the case of Los Angeles, this is true despite the presence of a strong black mayor and the support of most of the liberal citizenry. Hispanics and Asians have become more visible than in past years. The future of these blocs of power appears formidable. They will be less sensitive to the traditional role of black political power, even though they so far have ridden on its coattails. Waiting in the wings are the Korean-Americans, who are just now waking up to the realities of minority politics in America. So the black community in the inner city, where poverty reigns, can expect to have a very difficult time in the future, because for them there is little evidence that they even have much of a future.

But this much has not changed. I was amused at the experience of a white reporter for a major magazine, who, during the riots, arrived in the liberal city of San Francisco and proceeded to a troubled spot to record the scene for his publication. He arrived at the right place at the wrong time. He became the victim of mass police arrests. He found himself handcuffed and chopped in the groin by a female cop. Thirty-three hours and several police lockups later, he recorded this warning from a fellow inmate: "I'm concerned this is just the beginning of a period in America . . . that allows the police to revoke any rules. How do you distinguish between what happened in the Mission District [in San Francisco] and what happens in some Third World countries where people can be arrested just because they happen to be in the wrong place at the wrong time?" (*Business Week*, 18 May 1992, p. 48).

The racial identity of this inmate—a businessman—is not revealed in the article, but if he is white he has just been introduced to a reality faced by black men all the time. He has just become a black man, and we welcome him into this elite and somewhat exclusive company.

I fear that Los Angeles '92 *is* but a prelude to similar revolts throughout the country and, for that matter, around the world. From Paris, France, to Brixton, England, governments are gearing up to prevent the poor and disenfranchised from violent urban uprising. In the United States, it is just a matter of time until some cop blows it again in his or her treatment of a black person, probably a black man. Whether or not the incident is captured on video, it will trigger the next round of urban turmoil.

Sadly, not many people in this country seem to believe this. I recall speaking with a friend in Atlanta, a successful businessman and the father of two children. He lives in the relative safety of a nearby suburb, but he has not lost his conscience or his commitment to justice. He knows what he owes his children and is working on ensuring that they not be bigots. But like so many white people of similar conviction—and who, like him, may also be Christians—he attends a church where such things as riots in distant places are not mentioned: not even on the Sunday after Los Angeles burned and fourty-five people lost their lives. My friend asked one of his pastors for some explanation of this omission in the Sunday services. The pastor responded, "It's a matter of eschatology."

Well, it is not easy to know what some conservative believers mean by eschatology, especially in Atlanta. My guess is that it would not relate to the housing needs of black citizens there. In a major exposé in 1988, the city's major newspaper revealed that segregation in housing was rampant in the metropolitan area. And it was and is not relegated to low-income housing. To the contrary, segregated housing policies and patterns are most likely to be found at the middle- to upper-middle-income levels. The bottom of the ladder poses no threat to racists who live in more comfortable levels or to those who serve their interests in banks and other lending institutions. Bill Dedman reported after a study that "whites receive five times as many home loans from Atlanta's banks and savings and loans as blacks of the same income—and that gap has been widening each year." How big is that lending pie? It was 6.2 billion dollars over a period of six years. According to the study, most loans went to all-white neighborhoods, integrated neighborhoods followed, and all-black neighborhoods were dead last. The case of Michael Lomax is instructive. Lomax, one of the city's major political leaders, lived in a nearly all-black neighborhood. He ran for mayor in 1989. But even he could not escape the influence of the lending policies. Said

Lomax, "If I, a powerful black elected official, can't get a loan, what black person can?"

Race is the chief factor in this injustice. "Race—not home value or household income—consistently determines the lending patterns of Atlanta's largest financial institutions," the report said. Not surprisingly, no one is to blame. Frank Burke, chairman and CEO of Bank South, said,

> The numbers you have are damning. Those numbers are mind-boggling. You can prove by the numbers that the Atlanta bankers are discriminating against the central city. It's not a willful thing. The banks really are considered the pillars of the community. If somebody walks in and applies, they'll get fair treatment.

If "banks are considered pillars of the community," you can bet that bankers see themselves in the same light in spite of the scandals of recent years. Many of the them go to churches, and I catch a word from one or two of those pulpits via cable television every now and again. I have yet to hear one of those fancy preachers mention an issue such as discrimination in housing or racism in banking circles in the city. Some of these big congregations see themselves at the forefront of grand battles over biblical inspiration in seminaries and universities. It makes a man wonder, especially if he is black and looking for help for his family, if the issue all these years in conservative circles has really been about inerrancy. After all, it doesn't matter what theory of inspiration prevails in the absence of a commitment to apply what the Bible teaches.

The *Atlanta Journal-Constitution* study was a landmark report because of its sophistication. If done elsewhere, the results would very likely be similar all across the country. From West Hollywood to Yonkers, New York, the word from professionals is, "Housing discrimination is alive and well. The style has changed; it's gone underground." Of course, discrimination in housing is aimed at persons on factors other than race: age, marital status, physical handicaps, sexual orientation, or whether one has children. But by far, racial discrimination leads all other "reasons" for denial of housing.

There is evidence of discrimination in the field of education as well. The National Center for Education Information

(NCEI) revealed in 1988 that white males hold the majority of high-paying jobs in the American educational system. In a survey of more than 3,000 public school administrators, the Center found that more than 95 percent of the superintendents and 76 percent of the principals were white males. Most women are not surprised to be told this, since it has been common knowledge for years that the system has been run by a group of good ole boys—good ole white boys, to be exact. When the Los Angeles school board looked for a new district superintendent in 1987, it bypassed Latino and black candidates to hire a white male from Florida. The salary was $141,000 per year.

The kicker in the NCEI study is that whites held the high-paying jobs as principals even in neighborhoods dominated by so-called minorities—this at a time when the issue of role models in schools was being championed by some of these same educators. What does this say to black people? "Be like Mike. Be like Cliff Huxtable. Be like Claire. Be like Clarence. But don't be like us. These jobs are for an insular few. We know what's best for y'all."

I suppose that my Atlanta friend's pastor, by "eschatology," meant something having to do with end-time goings-on: wars and rumors of war and so forth. This pastor and his church no doubt were in total support of the war efforts of Reagan and Bush during the past decade. Well, pastor, if you want a war, stick around: There are any number of disenfranchised people—black and white—in and around Atlanta whose rage, once triggered, will give you a war to singe the hair of any pastor in the suburbs. And no ballyhoo about the Olympics or a Super Bowl will avert it.

There is one more thing the riots of '92 gave me occasion to ponder: the relevance of modern-day evangelicalism. I know the term is a broad one, but here I mean primarily that cluster of organizations with headquarters in Wheaton, Illinois, or Colorado Springs, two centers of so-called evangelical missions activity. I have in mind all those agencies that for so many years have defined orthodoxy and evangelistic practice, who have wrestled—sometimes valiantly—to define an evangelical theology for the church. I mean the network of saints who look at the world through blue eyes and tell the rest of us what they see and how it is to be understood.

The resources of my brethren—and a few sisters—are formidable both in human and economic terms. Influence among them and channeled through them is even more impressive. Some of them can pick up the phone and reach whoever is in the White House, and I suspect they can get a former President off his horse long enough to talk. With all the stored-up influence and IOU's these people have going for them, it would seem possible that they could have predicted an urban explosion in some major city. After all, the rumblings were there; a big one was as predictable as anything from a seismic center at Cal Tech.

But there were no warnings, no urgings to prepare, no emergency units available to the churches in the event of an explosion. Conferences were still being held. Pastors from mega-congregations were still convening in mountain settings to harangue seminaries for being irrelevant and to plan strategies for getting bigger and better. No black pastors were present at these gatherings, of course, even though their churches were "mega" before church-growth experts coined the phrase. The city was not on the agenda of those who convened the conferences, perhaps because their churches are not in cities.

Today, being that they are a bit older and a lot fatter, I look for my evangelical colleagues in different places whence I did in the sixties. I know they are not in the city, so I look for them in departments of urban studies at the undergrad and graduate levels. I expect them to be leading the parade in their seminaries to prepare future leaders to meet the challenge presented by an urban world; to develop concentrations in special programs up to the Ph.D. in how to think theologically in an urban community; to be leading the way in considering how worship and evangelism and preaching can be combined with community organization so that marginal people will have hope. And I keep looking to see if evangelical youth ministries will come up with something radical enough to snatch the souls of urban youth from the vice-grip of Minister Farrakhan and his minions. Of course, it will always be easier to raise money for youth ministries aimed at Russia or Hungary these days, but I keep looking.

Yet I must give credit where it is due. My impression is

that my evangelical friends responded with more strength in L.A. in the nineties than in Detroit in the sixties. The same may be true when the next blast rocks the Motor City. In Los Angeles, people could be seen sweeping up the mess, caring for the bereaved, and encouraging the victims of the disaster. Food poured in from all over by the truckload. Thousands of dollars were sent to key churches to assist their leaders in the recovery efforts. Thousands of dollars came from Korean evangelical churches.

Not that anybody knew whence the help arrived. If I lived in Central Los Angeles and had been wiped out, I'm not sure I would care who wrote the check or where a friendly face came from. I would probably not stop to read the label on the box. Who in West L.A. ever heard of evangelicals anyway? Baptists they know; Methodists—African Methodists, at least—they know; Catholics and Pentecostals they know. But who are evangelicals? Who under these circumstances cares?

Though I am thankful for the help many evangelicals provided to ease the pain, the end point of my pondering on contemporary evangelicalism is disappointment. I expected more because, like their politically conservative counterparts, they said they had more to give. They were supposed to know more of the answers because they had learned to ask better questions after the debacle of a spent liberalism. I expected more because there has come to be an acceptance of the notion that conservative theology automatically translates into conservative politics and social agendas that sound impressive. By now, I thought, my evangelical colleagues would have put it together better, would have come up with a marriage of their theology and their political ideology, laid it alongside the heartbreak of the city, and carved out some outposts of the Kingdom there.

Those outposts are there. But their leaders won't be invited to the latest gatherings of the evangelical club. Those outposts are led by a new breed, and they have yet to be discovered. That may not be a bad thing either.

Chapter Two

Black Male: Gorilla in the Mist

> *The record before this Commission reveals that the causes of recent racial disorders are embedded in a massive tangle of issues and circumstances—social, economic, political, and psychological—which rise out of the historical pattern of Negro-white relations in America. Of these, the most fundamental is the racial attitudes and behavior of white Americans toward black America* (U.S. Riot Commission Report, 1968).

"Mandingo is too dumb to go into shock." These words, extracted from recorded conversations within the Los Angeles Police Department, are references to Rodney King, alias "Mandingo," and a separate incident in which a black man was shot several times. That black man, according to recorded police conversations, was "too dumb to go into shock." Police Sgt. Stacey Koon, who labeled the King beating a "group beat," claims that the very sight of King gyrating with his hands on his buttocks before a female officer at the time of the arrest was reminiscent of old plantation sexual encounters between blacks and whites. "In society there's the sexual prowess of blacks on the old plantations of the South and intercourse between blacks and whites on the plantation. And that's where the fear comes in" (Sgt. Stacey Koon, unpublished manuscript, quoted in the *Los Angeles Times*, 16 May 1992).

Rodney King as "Mandingo." So the female cop, gun in hand, was fearful of this menacing black man, armed with a handful of buttocks. Thus Sergeant Koon begins the legitimating of the atrocity recorded on videotape on March 3, 1991, by George Holliday. Eighty-one seconds of hell.

Koon was acquitted of any responsibility in the beating, although he was the senior officer in charge. The actions of the officers were simply a matter of self-defense, and their remarks, clearly racist in nature, were merely the expressions of cops under pressure. Nothing personal or racist intended.* As one defense lawyer put it, the police were simply engaging in "careful police work." One juror expressed puzzlement over all the fury because, after all, "not much damage was done."

But the reference to black sex is straight out of Dixie and a thousand lynch-crazed mobs. According to Koon, this beating was in the defense of white womanhood: not just that of the female officer at the time but, by extension, all white women in society.

But it is not Sgt. Stacey Koon who evokes the most serious references to racist ideology in the service of law and order. That honor belongs to the Republican state representative from Louisiana's former 81st District. David Duke is handsome, suave, and convincing, especially when denying he is a racist. He ran for the presidency and, failing that, for governor. A former aide to Duke, Beth Rickey, after a long briefing early in their association, said, "He's very, very good. He kinda gets you. It's scary. He didn't come right out and start talking about Nazis right away. He tries to appeal to your sense of unfairness, the welfare system, and then gradually he starts reeling you in. 'Well, you know,' he finally says, 'it's the Jews.'"

---

*Officer Henry J. Cousine, one of forty-four LAPD police officers on the Christopher Commission's "problem officer" list, supports his former boss, Sergeant Koon. "I have a lot of respect for Sergeant Koon," says Cousine in an October 1992 interview. Then, commenting on the King incident, Cousine criticizes other officers involved in the beating: "They were swinging their batons like little girls. They should have laid some good chops on him. Three or four good chops. Chop! Chop! And that would have been the end of it" (*Los Angeles Times*, 4 October 1992, A35).

Duke is anti-Semitic and anti-black. More significant in the long run, he is also pro-white. Here are some typically Dukian remarks as recorded in November 1989. On Hitler: "I wouldn't say that Hitler was right on race, but I do believe that there are genetic differences between races and that they profoundly affect culture." (At the time, Duke kept a copy of *Mein Kampf* in his office.) And in the same breath, he said this on abortion: "But I'm opposed to abortion on moral grounds in other aspects because nature doesn't select that way. Nature gives people a chance, so maybe the way we should select [is] to let people go forth in life and just don't have programs that encourage them to reproduce like we do, in terms of the structure of the welfare system." Warming to his subject, Duke offered his version of a final solution: "We do feel an ideal—possibly an impossible ideal—would be geographic separation of the races either within this country or on an extra-continental basis. . . . geographic separation could include neighborhoods, could include anything. And I specifically say we're not trying to ship them back to Africa; I'm saying that a possible solution is that. That may be a possible solution" (*Indianapolis Star*, 14 January 1990, F5).

Clearly, black people are the targets of Duke's separatist ideology. The operative word is "anything." Any Jew in the world would know what that word can mean. Any racist South African would know its meaning, as would any victim of any apartheid-like system anywhere in the world. Duke is a dangerous man, not because he is a former grand wizard of the Knights of the Ku Klux Klan, nor because as a college student he held membership in a neo-Nazi organization. Not even because of his subsequent leadership of the National Association for the Advancement of White People. All this he dismisses as an exercise in youthful indiscretion. He is dangerous, not because of what he was, but because of what he still is. He has not been given enough of the sustained media exposure he deserves. The press covered him while he was hot, but promptly went to sleep after he lost the gubernatorial election in Louisiana in 1991. This is to be expected from a media system dominated by whites who do not feel threatened by an ex-Nazi. From the perspective of those who do feel threatened, there is no such thing as an ex-Nazi who can be safely ignored.

Perhaps more significantly, Duke represents danger because he clearly touched the nerve of many white Americans.
They responded to his ideas by sending him campaign money,
in amounts not yet fully recorded. His aim was to qualify for
federal matching funds. To do so, he needed to attract five
thousand voters in each of twenty states with contributions of
250 dollars or less. In fact, money came from fifty states, and
only 17 to 18 percent came from Louisiana. That done, all Duke
had to do was sustain his momentum by winning at least 10
percent of the votes in two successive primaries and the 13.8
million dollars in federal monies was his.

There is plenty of evidence that suggests that Duke is
really not interested in winning political office as a primary
goal. An article by Ralph Kinsey Bennett is a case in point. In a
revealing conversation between his former campaign director
and Duke, Robert Hawk recalls his shock at hearing Duke
admit that his real goal was not winning the Presidency if he
ran for that office. His real goal, according to Hawk, was the
money such a campaign could bring to his personal coffers. As
Duke put it to Hawk, "Man, that'd be clear money" ("Racial
Politics for Money," *Reader's Digest*, March 1992, pp. 43–48).

Bennett does not say whether Duke actually qualified for
federal funds. But Duke did generate more than 100,000 new
names for his computer-based propaganda machine. The man
can attract voters—more than 39 percent of the vote in his bid
for the governor's office. He is the point man for a nationwide
network of racist organizations and fellow travelers, often
directed by sophisticated young lawyers in three-piece suits.
Duke declared himself a Republican on the eve of qualifying for
the presidential primaries. The local party organization, never
known for its willingness to tackle a tough moral issue related
to racism, waffled in the face of the young man's challenge.
They never did challenge his constituents on this key issue. The
national party was not impressive in this regard, either. Oh,
speeches were made. President Bush screwed up his best
tough-guy image and hurled righteous invective at the notion
that racism could be tolerated within the ranks of the GOP.
That said, it was back to business.

Of course, there is a world of difference between Mr. Bush
and David Duke, or between former President Reagan and

Duke. Nothing in the Reagan-Bush record, either personal or in terms of the Republican party, reveals an ideology of racism such as characterizes David Duke.

But the party is about politics, and Republicans, no less than football coaches, know that second place is worse than kissing your sister. Winning is everything, and in the Deep South, where a revival of the Republican party has clearly been evident, party leaders are slow to jump on the issue of racism. Furthermore, the GOP was not in any position to answer the young candidate on the issues because both Ronald Reagan and George Bush won office by trumpeting the same issues— abortion, welfare, crime, unwed mothers, affirmative action— and appealing to the latent racism of the white working class. The difference is that poor Mr. Duke hasn't yet figured out how to finance fancier speechwriters. Patrick Buchanan was already employed, working on his own version of the same ideology.

That ideology is the ideology of white supremacy, and if it does not come across as white supremacist ideology, it is heard as pro-America rhetoric, and that means "white America." It can be easily appealed to. All a candidate needs is a black male to target: a Willie Horton. Beth Rickey is right in asserting her personal view that "Republicans set the tone for making racism acceptable through the Reagan years and through Bush's campaign for president with the Pledge of Allegiance and all that Willie Horton stuff." And that from a woman who has been a Republican activist since she was fourteen years old. Or consider this from an Afrikaner journalist as quoted in Studs Terkel's recent chronicle of race relations in the United States:

> Being from South Africa, I am obsessed with race. Any chance remark registers with me. Click. I just sense the whole *zeitgeist* has changed since Ronald Reagan was elected. In 1979, I ran into very few who expressed antagonism to black claims for restitution. Now you hear it at dinner parties, without any embarrassment. I met country-club patricians who were as outspoken in their racism as their blue-collar counterparts. You hear the litany, wholly uninvited (*Race* [New York: New Press, 1992], intro., p. 5).

At least David Duke is easy to figure. He spares us from having to deal with subtlety. Simply put, he believes that there are people—notably Blacks and Jews—who are racially "different," hence inferior. He is a racist on both the personal and social levels, viewing black people as possessing certain genetic differences that significantly define their behaviors and cultures. He then argues that such differences ought to require that such groups be segregated from white society. Segregation based on perceived genetic differences: It makes no difference to people who hold these views that such constructs were long ago dismissed by responsible scientists and researchers. Finally, it is obvious that the man from Louisiana would put into law what already exists in practice. That is, he would like to translate individual attitudes of racism, often based on spurious notions of genetic differences, into institutional forms.

This kind of racism could be understood as a new twist on "America first" ideology, which has a long history. For ultimately, racism in any form is an ideology, which is why it is so difficult to counter with facts. Some of us hear it in the endless rounds of "Japan bashing" by U.S. automobile executives. The talk is not just about who is making automobiles where.

Nor are racist views confined to the South. Indeed, they may have a wider appeal in the industrial North than in the agrarian South. A 1990s version of George Wallace might very well feel at home in the suburbs around Detroit and Milwaukee. Certainly he would among "skinheads" in Oregon and Idaho and perhaps even among out-of-work auto workers in Van Nuys, California. The Republican party—perhaps not always intentionally—has reaped the political fruits of racist attitudes. And as long as voters continue to put the party before the country and privilege before principle, Republicans have a secure future.

The typical racist behavior is more refined and thus more subtle than the blatant examples demonstrated by David Duke. Contemporary racism is not a matter of an elitist class shunning inferior people. Racism has a strong populist element that transcends social class. This is proven in part by the fact that Duke's views have touched a nerve across America.

The term *racism* is a recent addition to Western self-consciousness, but it is not new to the American experience. Race has been an issue in America ever since the Indians' unenlightened "immigration policy" by which Europeans reached these shores in large numbers. It has been the focal point of research and debate from Alexis de Tocqueville to Gunnar Myrdal to Arthur R. Jensen. It was an issue weighing heavily on the minds of Thomas Jefferson and George Washington long before it received the attention of the Rail Splitter from Illinois.

The contradictions between the words and the works of Thomas Jefferson perhaps best epitomize the dilemma of white Americans in his day—a dilemma that persists to this day. Jefferson unequivocally laid out what this country stood for in regard to human relations: "All people are created equal, and endowed by their creator with certain inalienable rights." He claimed that these truths were "self-evident." And in the meaning ascribed to these words by the Enlightenment, it would seem that the great farmer-statesman believed that all people ought to know this by nature and act accordingly.

But Jefferson had great difficulty applying his supposedly enlightened thought to slaves. He doubted their capacity to benefit from the civilizing experiment of Western thought and politics. Black people had bodies, but not brains. He proved the former by his sexual relations with a black slave woman, the significance of which was captured by historian Page Smith: "Thomas Jefferson, the great expositor of democracy, the prototype of the rational enlightened man, was in fact a slave holder, a brilliant emotional genius whose common-law wife was a slave, his dead wife's half sister" (*The Shaping of America*, vol. 3 [New York: Viking Penguin, 1989], intro., p. xiv). As for the intellectual capacities of black people, all Jefferson could offer was the vague hope that someday it might be proved that slave people could be civilized.

Most white people of the day held the same sentiments, and even those committed to the propagation of the Gospel became convinced that the best solution to the problem of slavery would be to send the slaves back to Africa. That would accomplish at least three goals: It would possibly aid in converting the Africans there; it would give the country some breathing room to sort out its ambiguity regarding its cultural ideology; and it would rid the nation of this "troublesome presence," as one historian called African slaves.

Throughout the history of this country, white European-Americans have had a difficult time coming to grips emotionally with the presence of the nonwhite male. The tension started with the native American and continues right up to the latest man of color to get off the plane. The man from Africa has been a particularly troubling presence. Black people, male and female, have shared in the indescribable pain of the American experience. But the racist policies inherent in our political and social systems have fallen with measured weight upon the black male. American history is laced with the machinations of white males against black males. Lynchings, beatings, drownings, political disenfranchisement, discrimination in the workplace, poor education, balconies in churches, and a thousand other contrived policies and practices have had a part in keeping the black male presence at a comfortable distance.

The atrocities began in Africa, of course, and while it is true that Africans were part of the conspiracy, they never defined fellow Africans in subhuman terms. In any case, the question of Africans' duplicity in the slave trade has nothing to do with what happened after the ships left the harbor. African tribalism had no part in the bestiality that characterized European-style slavery.

But, you ask, slavery is over now, isn't it? This question reminds me of the question on the bumper sticker that reads, "We're having fun now, aren't we?" Not really. Who could, with a straight face, contend that black men are no longer the objects of scorn, suspicion, and political disenfranchisement? Though the tactics have become more subtle, society still sends a clear message to black males that they are guilty before proven innocent. Not that the message is always subtle: Police and local sheriffs have been invested with considerable power to inflict suffering and intimidation upon black men whenever or wherever or under whatever circumstances they deem necessary. Any conversation with black men anywhere in the country—or even with white people who have experienced the black urban scene—will confirm this assertion even to the most hardened skeptic. The stories sound the same. Police surveillance has now become part of unofficial governance in urban America. While this is justified to some extent, given the sophistication and ubiquity of the new underworld in our

urban settings, it does not account for the seemingly pur-
poseless snooping into the lives of ordinary black males.

This suffocating police presence helps explain the black
response to the Simi Valley verdict. Black males correctly
perceive that the behavior of white cops toward them could not
happen with such consistency if white people did not condone
it. Indeed, moving the trial to Simi Valley sent the message to
black people that white America *does* condone police brutality,
that black men still threaten white America, even if white kids
wanna be like Mike.

Ordinary blacks who struggle to overcome the effects of
prejudice and discrimination on their lives receive little inspiration from a recitation of a list of those black men and women
who have "made it" in society. Cliff and Claire Huxtable made
it. As providence would have it, on the night Los Angeles was
torched, this famous fictional family was winding down its
long-standing love affair with family life in urban America. A
poke at the TV's remote button and one experienced the
emotional whiplash between the family values Bill Cosby
created and the ear-splitting screams from the streets.

Some crack Ph.D. student could make a valuable contribu-
tion with a dissertation comparing the Huxtable family with the
Bunker family created by Norman Lear in the seventies. In
many ways, the struggle for America's soul is typified in the
prototypes of Cliff and Archie: upwardly mobile African-Americans—doctors, lawyers, business people—and blue-collar
white Americans feeling that "those people" somehow have no
right to be where they are, that they got there because of
affirmative action. What prototypes, Cliff and Archie!

Protoypes, by definition, represent a sort of heightened
reality. The true reality is not so blatant or extreme. Unfortunately, too many black men tend to see too many white people
as Archie. They see him in Simi Valley, of course, but also on
Wall Street, in executive offices of most professional sports
teams, in mansions where governors live, and until recently, at
Parker Center in L.A., where the top cop had his office. Darryl
Gates as Archie Bunker. Sgt. Stacey Koon as Archie Bunker.
Patrick Buchanan as Archie Bunker. Black men live in a world
full of Archie Bunkers. They occupy faculty positions at the
university or the seminary and are well represented in the

student body. They are in the recording business, including that peculiar group of record entrepreneurs who produce so-called Christian contemporary music. A black man would look in vain to find a brother writing regularly for a major evangelical magazine. By now he is tired of white believers interpreting the world for him, so he rarely reads the magazines anyway. The issues confronting black men in society, even Christian black men, do not seem to interest the majority of God's people. This assessment brings to mind the words of Samuel F. Yette, who pulled the scab off race relations when he argued in 1971 that black people are obsolete in America. Yette's premise was that by the end of the sixties one issue had emerged among black people and that issue was survival. "Examination of the problem," he argued, "must begin with a single overpowering socioeconomic condition of the society: black Americans are obsolete people."

A talented journalist for *Newsweek* at the time his book was published, Yette pressed his case that

> black Americans have outlived their usefulness. Their raison d'etre to this society has ceased to be a compelling issue. Once an economic asset, they are now considered an economic drag. The wood is all hewn, the water all drawn, the cotton all picked, and the rails reach from coast to coast. The ditches are all dug, the dishes all put away, and only a few shoes remain to be shined.

To Yette, "the most frightful and pressing question facing America in the '70s" was, "Can black people survive as men and women and not as chattel?" (*The Choice: The Issue of Black Survival in America* [Silver Spring, Md.: Cottage Books, 1988]).

The issue remains unresolved in the nineties—but not so much at the top levels of society, where the very talented few within black America have found a niche. Like their white counterparts, these people have been able to take advantage of educational advances to distance themselves from the previous limitations of work options. In many sectors those options are in decline for people who lack training. The editors of *Fortune* contend that "the new fault line splitting America into two nations, rich and poor, does not run between blacks and whites. Rather, it increasingly separates well-educated, skilled professionals of all races from the rest of society" (1 June 1992, p. 42). The editors admit, however, that this situation has handicapped black males more than others in the work force. And the best explanation is education. By and large, black males simply have not been retained in the educational systems at any level.

The *Fortune* article goes on to offer some intriguing ideas and analysis despite sounding like the establishment journal it is. There is no mention, for example, that racism in hiring or promotion has anything to do with unemployment or the loss of millions of dollars among blacks through underemployment. Christopher Jencks, noted sociologist from Northwestern University, comes closest to the point when he argues, "If we want to reduce the poverty, joblessness, illiteracy, violence, or despair of the so-called underclass we will surely need to change our institutions and attitudes in hundreds of small ways, not one big way" (Ibid., p. 48). Jencks's plan to get black people off welfare is impressive, well balanced, and compassionate. He is obviously correct in asserting that people on welfare need new rules to live by. "A successful policy has to begin by abandoning the myth that poor families can support themselves entirely by working. Unskilled single mothers can't support their families on $5 an hour" (Ibid., p. 48).

But the same magazine is quick to point out that black males are more likely to end up unemployed than their white counterparts, more likely to end up in prison, especially between the ages of twenty and twenty-nine, and certainly more likely to be murdered. Something is clearly terribly wrong, and if Yette's assertion—now nearly twenty years old—is not close to correct, how does one account for these disparities?

The problem with making such an assertion today is that recent studies seem to run counter to it. Yet the National Research Commission admits that no one has done much research on discrimination in the workplace and, it would seem, even less on discrimination against black males. Their "inference" (their word, not mine) from available work is that there is not as much discrimination as existed before the decade of the seventies and that existing discrimination has less impact on blacks in dollar terms then before. They also conclude that black women experience no more discrimination than white women, but experience considerable discrimination compared with both black and white men. Most of this research has been done by the Equal Employment Opportunity Commission and the friendly people over at the U.S. Department of Justice. Sources aside, these "inferences" do not jibe with black people's perceptions of reality. Not surprisingly, among black people the sources alone are enough to trigger suspicion.

When reading Barlett and Steele's analysis of what went wrong with America, I couldn't help but wonder where black people were in the research, especially black men. The focus of their book (*America: What Went Wrong?* [Kansas City: Andrews & McMeel, 1992]) is on middle-class Americans, and although they are barely visible in the book, there are plenty of them in black communities and scattered throughout the labor force. They, no less than their white counterparts, are being slowly drained of economic viability.

The omission is significant especially because there is no such thing as a secure black middle class. If white middle-class people are losing their grip on the American dream, black middle-class status is even more tenuous. To be sure, many blacks have prospered during the past twenty-five years, and this growth is one of the great triumphs of the nation in recent history. But a closer look reveals that black men, even at this level, still make less money than their white counterparts with equal education. Black college graduates end up making only slightly more than white males who only finished high school. The bottom line is that many blacks are better off only when compared with the past or with other black people whose education was curtailed at lower levels. Black men of equal talent and educational levels seem destined never to catch up with their white male counterparts.

All this was not exactly supposed to be the result of more than fifty years of government attempts to ensure equal access to the workplace for all Americans. In a fine and balanced piece on this subject, *Business Week* magazine chronicled the many battles in government and business to end discrimination at all levels of corporate and commercial life in America. It is a grisly story for the most part, yet there have been some startling breakthroughs in recent years. Still, corporate America is segregated at the top. "Nearly 97% of senior executives in the biggest U.S. companies are white, and while blacks make up 12.5% of the private sector work force, only 5% of all professionals are black" (*Business Week*, 8 July 1991, p. 52).

Some would agree that affirmative action is the cause for much of this disparity: If left to themselves, corporate America would have solved the inequities in the workplace without liberal government interference. Of course this issue is complicated. Any number of forces conspire to frustrate Americans of all races these days. But white people do not need to list racism as one of them. Affirmative action will do. As *Business Week* points out, only one in ten whites say they have been victims of reverse discrimination. This is a considerable number of people, but the kind of discrimination encountered by respondents is unclear. White people could hardly experience "reverse discrimination" because they are white. They are discriminated against because of a system their fathers had ignored, and finally, in the name of justice, the chickens came home to roost at the son's henhouse.

But discrimination is discrimination, and it is always wrong. No doubt affirmative action has been wrongly applied in some cases. Its ultimate purpose, however, is to counter the effects of discrimination. To argue against affirmation action as a concept is to presuppose that racism has ceased to exist. In this regard, it has puzzled me for years why white people should be concerned about reverse discrimination when the same people have easily tolerated, without conscience, all sorts of discrimination against minorities. Maybe affirmative action will result in a black person's getting a job for which he or she may not be qualified. But black people have been around long enough to know that many jobs are held by white people who are not qualified. They either were the bosses' sons or knew somebody who knew somebody.

The same reality exists in Christian circles if you respect the majority view among minority Christians. Take a look at Christian colleges and seminaries and see where the minorities are placed in the system. The scene will look a lot like corporate America. In most cases, the highest-ranking black executive will be in charge of personnel or recruitment. The same would be true of major evangelistic associations. I learned long ago that these groups were not serious about reaching minorities. I discovered this by examining their hiring practices, by watching to see whose sons got hired before any public notice ever went out, by watching the president and founder pass the buck on race concerns to some junior executive, knowing full well that to do so would send the signal that this issue was not a top priority.

And many of these are the leaders of organizations who are cranking it up to reach the world by the year 2000. The world they are trying to reach is made up mostly of people who are not represented in their top echelon of strategists and decision makers.

Admittedly, some of this is due to past injustice—the sins of the fathers. Segregation at evangelical colleges and seminaries, the often cool and hostile attitudes of many who allowed blacks to attend, the refusal to employ graduates from these schools in any significant leadership roles—these practices account for much of the white predominance in evangelical institutions.

Sociologist Joe Feagin has written about the trends in recent research among certain academics, black and white. According to Feagin, academics do not see racism as a significant factor in determining upward mobility in society. This conclusion is reflected in updated rhetoric: Terms such as "racism" and "institutionalized racism" have given way to references to "the underclass," "affluent black middle class," and "pathology of the black family." But black people don't read those journals catering to the cognoscenti. Nor did they listen much to the same ideas put forth in simpler terms by Patrick Buchanan during his aborted attempt in 1992 to gain the White House at their expense. But black people do talk with each other and with anyone else who will listen. And when they do, they talk about a different reality, identifying white racism as the underlying reason they are not making it.

Feagin is right in insisting that the current fascination among scholars to attempt to demonstrate that racism is not a significant factor smacks of a revised version of blaming the victims. Says Feagin: "I have found that only a few candid interviews with black Americans are needed to reveal to a white researcher how off the mark are mainstream notions of the declining significance of race and the prosperity of the advanced middle class" ("Point of View," *Chronicle of Higher Education*, 27 November 1991, A44). Even those blacks who seem well-off can tell more than a few horror stories about the psychological toll they have paid for their affluence.

For black males pursuing jobs, things look to get worse before they get better. They must compete for jobs not only with an increasing number of black women who want to enter the work force, but also with any number of other minorities. In California, minorities make up 44 percent of the work force, and competition for jobs is fierce in a state where the economy has gone flat. Predictably, those at the lower end of the educational scale are the most vulnerable, and economic realities will increasingly pit them against one another. Hispanic voices can already be heard complaining that black people are getting too much attention and more than their share of the affirmative-action pie. Blacks respond by asking where Hispanics were when all the civil rights marching was going on? Asians aren't saying anything, out loud at least. But they are working all hours to send their children to college. In this way they manage to transcend the debates other ministries engage in. They are not interested in *those* jobs anyway.

Increasingly, black and white intellectuals are arguing that the whole scheme of affirmative action—or to use the new phrase, "managing diversity"—is detrimental to all people concerned. According to the argument, it hurts those who are excluded as not being minorities, or at least not the right minority. It also hurts the beneficiary, who is left to wonder if he or she truly got hired on the basis of merit. These are fair and important concerns. Certainly black people with good jobs, especially at the executive level, can identify with the point. The higher up one goes today, the more he or she is concerned over the issue of merit. Even if this does not occupy conscious thought, there is always someone on the job to remind a person in subtle ways that he or she might be there because of one's race.

The truth is that blacks and Hispanics have always been willing to be hired or turned away based on merit. It was their experience of continual rejection without being given a chance to prove their merit that led to the corrective measure of affirmative action. They also know that white people, as the majority, already had their own unofficial affirmative-action program; in a system governed by whites, no laws were necessary. But if laws had been needed, white people would have responded in the same way that minorities have. They would have marched, burned buildings, and overturned a few squad cars. The history of the labor movement in this country proves that point conclusively.

There is something of a conspiracy against those who still insist that racism is a major contributing factor to black economic depression. Such people don't usually enjoy equal print space in the journals of the establishment. This condition reflects the legacy of the Reagan-Bush years. It was Bush who initially vetoed civil rights bills, thus carrying out the crusade against civil rights initiated by Reagan's point man, Ed Meese. We tend to forget that one of Reagan's first actions upon reaching the White House was to launch an assault upon the Civil Rights Commission. He succeeded in eviscerating a once-proud and effective instrument for justice in American society. One would suspect that this was an attempt to direct blame for the country's continuing racial ills away from white America. In reality, it was a mere payback. Reagan did not campaign among black people any more than George Wallace did; both knew that this is not where the country is. The country had turned conservative and anti-government, targeting especially those parts of the government responsible for forcing black children into their schools and for opening the way for black adults to compete for jobs through affirmative action.

Recall that Reagan came to power because of his ability to embarrass President Carter over the stalemate in the Middle East. Carter, perceived by his detractors as liberal on social issues, including racial matters, was painted as being soft on the Arab leadership in the Middle East. Even his disastrous rescue attempt of the Americans held hostage in Iran could not recast his image as a defender of America on foreign soil. One wonders what Reagan would have argued had those prisoners been black?

This is not to argue that Reagan's strategy was dictated by a personal racist ideology. There is no evidence for that— probably none could be developed that would pass any test for "evidence." No, he was simply trying to win a political battle, and he knew that white America was sick and tired of deferences paid to colored people anywhere in the world. White Americans wanted a leader for white America. Colored people had had their day long enough—off and on since Franklin Roosevelt.

The political strategy was to convince white America that a country such as this, with roots in Europe, had not business having its nose rubbed in dung supplied by Arabs.

During the Reagan era, we witnessed a reshaping of the Supreme Court based largely on white conservatives' perspective on political and social reality. We saw sustained and unremitting attacks on the agencies in the forefront of civil rights activities. Before Reagan left office, Bush adopted much the same strategy. After all, he must bear primary responsibility for exploiting racial attitudes for political gain by elevating a black ex-convict to infamy during the campaign of 1988. Willie Horton thus became a further symbol as to why the country must retain its more civilized roots in Euro-American culture and values. Reagan and Bush's policies were about values. But the values of black people had become suspect.

Both as Vice President and as President, Bush has consistently conveyed the view that positions associated with black people—in short, the liberal agenda—are well-nigh un-American. In running for the White House he made the dreaded "L-word" a new symbol of all that is wrong in the society. So the country saluted the flag and sent Dukakis home to his nearly bankrupt state. Black people showed no great passion either way because Dukakis didn't spend too much time on our side of town either. The jury is still out on William Clinton as of this writing.

The weight of this ideological assault, when translated into bottom-line job opportunities, fell most heavily on black males, who were simply not prepared to enter that competition. Now, as soon as he walks through the door, a black man is viewed as just another beneficiary of a quota system.

Not a lot has changed in the time that has passed between Watts 1965 and Los Angeles 1992. As a society, we are still doing splits, straddling the gulf between our moral sensibilities and our willingness to implement those values in concrete terms. "As the attitudinal data suggest, contemporary black-white relations fall between the overt racism of the past and an unambiguous commitment to full integration and equal opportunity," reports the team associated with the National Research Council (p. 138). This is a fancy way of saying that white people assent to equal treatment of blacks in the workplace and housing and schooling, but not in great numbers.

Unfortunately, the evangelical establishment is largely indistinguishable from much of white America. The evangelical world is prepared to deal with black men one at a time: If you don't foul up, or if you maintain a style acceptable to the majority, you can be more or less accepted. Not as a human being, of course, at least not in the fullest sense. As Sam Yette might say, blacks have a certain usefulness in the white evangelical culture. And as Gary Wills observed in the late sixties, "Americans do not like to think of their country as being white, but they are careful to keep it that way." A great line, and fully applicable to the turf occupied by early-nineties evangelicals.

Chapter Three

The Politics of Race and Class

Race is no longer a straightforward, morally unambiguous force in American politics; instead, considerations of race are now deeply embedded in the strategy and tactics of politics, in competing concepts of the function and responsibility of government, and in each voter's conceptual structure of moral and partisan identity (Thomas B. Edsall, *Atlantic Monthly*).

I have a confession to make: I am indebted to Ronald Reagan and George Bush for helping me understand something important. With the first and second coming of Mr. Reagan, I was forced to deal with emotions I now know were in the gut of most Americans during all those years the liberals ran things. I now know how they felt. Someone had stolen their country, and they wanted it back. Who had stolen it? Liberals using the poor, criminals, blacks, welfare mothers—that whole swath of humanity the Democrats subsidized through a thousand giveaway programs. Hardworking white Americans wanted their country back. With Reagan and Bush, they took it back and helped me get in touch with the feelings of others. Thanks, Mr. President.

But long before Reagan and Bush there was Richard Nixon. And before Nixon, the department store magnate from Phoenix. Barry Goldwater voted against the Civil Rights Act of 1964, making him perhaps the first Republican candidate in that era who was willing to stick his large chin out and let the liberals take a crack at it. Goldwater was steamrolled by Lyndon Johnson in the election of that year, one of the most lopsided elections in American history. Americans did not buy his extremist approach to the supposed defense of liberty.

Some political analysts argue that the '64 election was a turning point in American politics. Thomas Edsall claims it was the "first and last presidential election in which racial liberalism was politically advantageous." Ever since, politicians' use of race and racial issues has virtually become an art form. When performed by some craftsmen of the Right, race has been a devastatingly effective political tool. In an article in *Atlantic Monthly*, Edsall writes,

> Race plays an important role in defining liberal and conservative ideologies. It shapes the presidential coalitions and platforms of the Democratic and Republican parties. Racial overtones underlie concerns over taxes and crime, often driving a wedge through alliances of the working classes and the poor. These same overtones, subtle though they may be, provide both momentum and vitality to the drive to establish a national majority inclined by income and demography to support policies benefiting the affluent and the upper middle class. In terms of public policy, many would argue that race has played a critical role in the creation of a political system that has tolerated, if not contributed to, the growing disparity between rich and poor over the past fifteen years (Thomas Byrne Edsall with Mary D. Edsall, "Race," *Atlantic Monthly*, May 1991, p. 53).

A climate wherein race plays a part in political strategy is something Ronald Reagan inherited and, to an appreciable degree, helped advance. Reagan was a handsomer George Wallace, a more photogenic Richard Nixon, a much more savvy Gerald Ford. A male version of Margaret Thatcher without the Iron Lady's brilliance. Reagan and his ideologues outmaneuvered the Democrats at every political turn, capitalizing on the inability of the latter to give up what they thought was the high ground of social transformation achieved throughout most of the seventies. Reagan's people knew that even most Democrats by 1980 had had more than enough social transformation.

By then, most Democrats felt betrayed by their party, which in their judgment had been taken over by people who no longer represented the core values of America. Among those people were blacks, feminists, welfare mothers, and, later, gays as they pressed their claims for inclusion in the company of cultural outcasts. Auto workers in Detroit, whose fathers had refused to allow a Republican to sit on the platform at Labor Day celebrations in the good old days, incited the wrath of their old men by voting in the new order. Most of them have never returned to the Democratic fold. What a revolution!

I am also indebted to George Bush for giving us Dan Quayle. After I got over the emotional shock of this odd choice, I watched Quayle schmaltz his way across the face of the earth, and I must say he has provided me with some comedic relief. By the time he paid his obligatory visit to Los Angeles in the wake of the riots, I had even gotten to like the man. Great smile, handsome in a soft, midwestern way. A family man with a passable golf swing. Religious, too, albeit in the mold of New Right fundamentalism. By the time the '92 campaign rolled into the scarred city, I had learned that Quayle's role in the Administration was to articulate the party strategy—a strategy that in effect called for bringing the country together by tearing it apart. The effect of his speeches was to pit women against women, rich against poor, employed against the unemployed, the elderly against the young. And he did it for the most part in the guise of family values and morality. Quayle became the point man in a new conservative moral crusade, a white-washed version of John the Baptist in a Brooks Brothers suit calling on common people and "Murphy Brown" to repent.

Vice President Quayle knew exactly why the uprising had happened in L.A.: Family values had disappeared in the country, especially black family values. Even though he chose fiction—a popular television show—for his illustration of declining moral values, single-parent families headed by women are a primary reality of the black "underclass." His words, of course, were not aimed directly at black people any more than Nixon aimed his law-and-order message at black people in the same city many years before. After all, Republicans haven't spoken *to* black people since Abe Lincoln. They do, however, speak *about* black people.

Quayle's message was ultimately meant for all those fine conservatives out there who continue to believe the country is shot to hell because the liberals still set the social agenda, an agenda that has allowed welfare mothers to leech off the government, has encouraged black women to bear children out of wedlock, and has opened the door for homosexuals to lobby for government handouts for AIDS research. It was a beautiful act. Had he stayed longer, Quayle might have been enshrined in cement on the Hollywood Walk of Fame.

But for millions of Americans, Quayle's speeches were not an act. He was speaking for them. And I confess that I am attracted to some of it. Something has gone terribly wrong in the country's moral orientation. Something is wrong in the black communities across the country when 60 percent of black children are born out of wedlock and when a disproportionate number of black males are in prison even if you allow for a certain degree of discrimination. Something is wrong when the country makes a hero of a wealthy and talented black athlete upon his so-called courageous admission that he has the AIDS virus, even though he was one of our most talented fornicators. No amount of applause on Arsenio Hall's late-night bash can dispel that issue.

But surely even Republicans know, as do their supporters in evangelical churches, that morality has taken a nose dive in white America also, all the way from Pennsylvania Avenue to Wall Street to Beverly Hills. Politicians talk selectively about declining morality. Most of the corruption among white elites is economic in nature, practiced by people and corporations whose coffers were oft times at the disposal of those leading the moral crusade. Nor do evangelicals talk much about greed. Sexual profligacy? Yes, especially when the offenders are televangelists and pastors. But greed is too American to criticize. Most of these high-class thieves are friends of those elected by people who voted their pocketbooks instead of their principles. And these wise guys in white shirts will live to steal again after they finish their brief stays at country-club prisons. From the back seats of their Mercedes limos, they will still confer their bullish attitudes on the business of America. No matter. Don't wait for Dan Quayle to address this sort of decline in values.

Quayle is talking to the crowd that cheers for all those black guys, and a few whites, who from one end of the country to the other muscle their way to titles in professional sports. In Detroit they are called Lions and Pistons, but those folks in the stands gave up on Detroit years ago. Let Mayor Coleman Young have the godforsaken place, and we will forgive Isiah Thomas for selling Toyotas as long as the games are played in Pontiac and Auburn Hills.

The Democratic party has played politics with race as well, though with different goals in mind. Democrats were responsible for the Voting Rights Act in 1965, which gave black people political legitimacy for the first time in the nation's history. But they did it with the consent of most Americans. After all, that is what this country is about. Democracy requires that all its citizens participate in the process; short of that, there is no true democracy. White Americans support these democratic values. But with the passage of civil rights legislation, their belief in democracy was tested by a growing sense that the Democrats were pushing goodness down their throats and perhaps going a bit too far in the name of democracy.

I believe the Edsalls are correct in arguing that it was Richard Nixon who discerned these feelings among the electorate sooner than most Republicans. George Wallace knew it better than his fellow Democrats. In the 1968 presidential election, Wallace bolted the Democratic party, which nominated Hubert Humphrey, and ran as the candidate of the American party. Together Nixon and Wallace garnered 57 percent of the tally. The winner, of course, was Nixon. Most disenchanted white Americans couldn't admit later to voting for a Southern, redneck racist. But in choosing Nixon they voted for what Wallace was really railing against: the heavy-handed, Washington-based liberalism of the Democrats. Wallace's states'-rights emphasis sounded to blacks for all the world like a euphemism for white supremacy, even though he vehemently denied that. In any case, to most blacks, Nixon and Wallace looked pretty much the same.

I recall seeing Governor Wallace in the spring of 1972 about a week before he was shot. Tom Skinner and I were conducting an evangelistic series in Flint, Michigan. Wallace was carrying his own crusade to the people who worked the factories in that General Motors town. I thought at the time he had a good chance of winning the state in the presidential primary. After all, the people who were making the cars from Detroit to Pontiac to Flint and even Lansing, the state capital, were downhome folks. Wallace loved to call them rednecks, and they didn't seem to mind. "Rednecks of the World Unite" might be an accurate paraphrase of his call to action. I was impressed with Wallace's smile as he shook my hand. As he looked me straight in the eye, he had to know without knowing me that I would not likely support his campaign in my home state. I didn't. He won anyway, as I figured he would. Twenty-four years later, a different George, more suave in his manner, has successfully appealed to the same disappointments, fears, and prejudices of the American people.

Reagan's advisors were in touch with the same feelings his Republican predecessors had touched. But by the time of his candidacy, these feelings were ready to explode. After taking office in 1981, Reagan promptly relieved some of the pressure by laying siege to the legislation that had caused so much anxiety and the agency that embodied it, the Civil Rights Commission itself. This legislation and that agency had come to symbolize for white, conservative America the extent to which liberals were prepared to give the country away to people who had not earned it.

But the real clincher in Republican racial politics was the gradual replacement of the remaining liberal judges on the Supreme Court. William Rehnquist is now the chief justice in a Reagan-Bush court committed to undoing, in the interests of conservative political ideology and with all eyes glued to their conservative constituencies, most of the gains achieved in civil rights over the past thirty years. True to form, George Bush used a black man to make the point that those who count in this country are those who have made it.

The selection of Clarence Thomas was calculated to send a message to black Americans that their best interests do not lie with the Democrats. "Read my lips," Bush seemed to be saying. "We know what's best for all of you. We have chosen a shining example of all that's good about the country. An example of hard work, up from poverty, a bright legal mind who has paid his dues. Rejoice!" Some black people did, especially those who were more interested in having a black person on the Court than in what that black person stood for. Most black people saw the selection for what it was, just another predictable choice of a white Easterner committed to making sure that the status-quo-politically-conservative concept of justice would be reinforced.

So far, Thomas has been running true to form, neck and neck with archconservative Antonin Scalia. Dubbed by some observers as the "D.C. Duo," they have argued that beating a handcuffed prisoner may not be a violation of the Eighth Amendment prohibition against cruel and unusual punishment. That this ruling was out of line is suggested by the ensuing rebuke that came from the other seven jurists in the Court.

Racial politics is nothing new to the American judicial system, including the Supreme Court. Nor are Republicans the only party whose politics has determined Supreme Court selections. But what is frightful about this Court is that it comes to power at a time of mean-spiritedness in the society. The country is emotionally off balance. We are in an in-between period in our history when old formulas have proved ineffective and new ideas and forms are not yet in place. Our politicians are largely bankrupt ethically, as evidenced by the rise of the ever-popular phenom who calls Texas home. No, I mean the billionaire businessman, Ross Perot. His presence in the presidential campaign of 1992 marked a change from past times when only black people knew that the choice in most election years was between a known devil and a suspected witch.

Now most Americans have come to similar conclusions. Thus the number of Americans who vote has dropped precipitously in recent years, especially in off-year elections, which are often the only ones where issues of substance get debated. The large voter turnout last November was a significant turnaround for the electorate, yet it remains to be seen if this interest can be sustained into the mid-nineties.

The growing disenchantment with the political system, laced with a streak of cynicism a mile wide, exposes the country to far-right influence at top levels. I have long felt that the late Saul Alinsky had it about right when he argued that as middle-class America went, so would go the country. By the time the middle class finally caught on that they—not blacks or the poor—were the real losers in the game of politics being played by their conservative benefactors, the country would move in one of two directions: either toward radical social reform or toward its own brand of American-style fascism. Alinsky said this in 1972.

Politics, of course, goes hand in hand with economics these days. And economics raises issues related to class. To be sure, sometimes politics appeals to local cultural values. Witness the varied attempts of the parties to tie into the fundamentalist moralities of the South, or the rancor in the South and West over the Establishment snobs from the Eastern seaboard. But ultimately politics is about money. Are you better off financially than you were four years ago today? That's what the typical American is interested in.

From the viewpoint of politicians, politics is also about making money. And getting elected. The two go hand in hand. That is part of the reason why the Republicans have enjoyed the edge in the White House. They have had more money than they knew what to do with, outspending their opponents by an average of 2 to 1 in the last few presidential election years.

Until recently, Republicans have also been more alert to the compulsions in America society than the Democrats have been. From Nixon to Bush they have slanted their campaign tactics to appeal to the basic fear in the culture that somehow people of color would gain an advantage in the marketplace over white people. The tactics have not always worked, because there remains a strong sense in the culture that equity should prevail as part of the American dream for everyone. This knowledge has kept many black people from total despair.

Democrats have operated in this arena, too, only with a reverse spin. They used people of color to shape social policy and to maintain control in Washington—if not the White House, at least in the Congress. These policies seem to have the right instincts behind them and have been perceived by most black people as having their best interests at heart.

If, in a previous time, the racial messages that underlie the political and economic debate were more subtle, today the veneer is off politics. Even the press has begun to refer to the "politics of race." Reagan, Bush, Newt Gingrich et al. may not be older clones of David Duke, but they could teach the young man a lesson or two about how to get elected without changing his positions. So could Jesse Helms, the U.S. Senator from North Carolina who trotted out his racist-oriented tactics when it became clear he could lose the 1990 election to a black man. His political gambit paid off.

What is there about the Grand Old Party that attracts it so to racialist inclinations within the country? For one thing, it has successfully plugged into the country's shift to a more conservative ethos. Democrats seemed reluctant to admit that they no longer represented the America that was saved by the New Deal. Reagan and his people knew it, however, and shaped a revised version of the New Deal, giving it a neo-conservative twist and aiming it squarely at white America's need to be *numero uno* in the world. Then they targeted the upper class as the focal point of the new movement, knowing it would be easy to convince the rest of us that if the upper crust prospered, prosperity would trickle down like water and the rising tide would raise all boats. White America, and a handful of black Americans with short memories, bought the package whole because there is a certain appeal to all Americans in the prospect of wealth, health, and happiness. The scheme failed for most Americans, but it did raise some beautiful yachts.

Another reason for the Republican edge is related to the relative ease with which right-wing groups have been able to identify their policies with patriotism. Conservatives have somehow found it easier than liberals to wrap themselves in the flag. Bush did it with his celebrated Pledge of Allegiance in the 1988 campaign, and who can forget Reagan's snappy salute as he alighted from his "copter"? Ronald Reagan as John Wayne. It played beautifully, a veritable top-level, real-life version of patriot games. Flags and salutes are really about old-fashioned American values, like motherhood, apple pie, and Chevrolets. They are about morals and hard work and an A-frame in the north woods. They are not about trying to understand and do something about crime and poverty, unwed mothers, and street gangs.

Before the '88 elections Jesse Jackson seemed to be the only politician who knew that the future of the Democratic party—indeed of the country—was in the hands of the "Rainbow" people. "Red and yellow, black, and white" became more than an innocuous children's chorus. These colors represented the new reality of America, especially urban America. The coalition has also included people from America's farm belt—Americans who have been losing their farms to agri-business and international mega-corporations as food and its production have become synonymous with politics and big money.

But ultimately the Democrats had only slightly more political space to offer Reverend Jesse than the Republicans did. If he had become the party's leader, it would have been the final signal to white Democrats that they had finally surrendered the whole thing to black people. Instead, the party cast its lot with an insipid white governor from New England. So the election of 1988 was about race, whether you rode an elephant or a donkey. Bush won because he "out-niggered" the Democrats. In 1992, he was still working on the formula. By ignoring the depression at the core of America's cities, he made it clear again that *that* issue was still about people of color. He made the point by keeping silent about it.

Nor could these same Democrats support Jackson in his attempts to inject himself into international politics. Jackson, perhaps the most astute tactician among Democrats, saw early on the racial implications of the United States' dealings with the Middle East. He knew that the stakes there were higher than the mere survival of Israel, and he knew that this country would have to move more in the direction of serious talks with Arab nations. It could not have escaped his eye that those nations were perceived to be more colored in the eyes of the elite cadre who run the State Department than were those people who called themselves Jews in Palestine. Jackson tested those waters in his successful attempt to rescue a downed American flyer. Taken captive by the Syrians, the pilot could have become another casualty in the hostage war, but Jackson went to Syria and secured his release. Was it significant that both Jackson and the pilot are African-Americans? Is it true that the only reason President Reagan did not receive the news of this transaction with joy is that Jackson worked outside official

State Department policy governing hostage issues? Or did Jackson's venture test the Administration's implicit racial boundaries?

After all, what would American foreign policy look like if an African-American became President? More specifically, what if that African-American were Jesse Jackson? Not even all black Americans were happy with that prospect. But that is not the point. The point is that in a system where race is such a factor in determining policy and international relations, a black man puts foreign policy into another realm. Think of the economic implications had Jackson been in office during the South African imbroglio. Could the State Department have so easily turned away Haitian refugees if a black man were in the White House? Or would Washington be as cozy with the Cuban community in Miami?* Given the attitude of the Jewish community toward Jackson, one can only imagine the paroxysms of grief that would have shaken those centers had he been elected. Add to all this the increase in racism throughout Europe aimed primarily at people of color and it becomes clear that the United States has a very long wait before it hails a black chief.

But Jackson's exclusion from the high ranks of the Democratic party is not nearly so risky as it seemed a year or so earlier. He represents the old order in the party. Bill Clinton represented the new order of younger pols. To succeed, they moved to the center in an effort to appeal to the larger mass of Americans: blacks, whites, and whoever else wants a better chance to make it in America. Jackson seems to represent another, older dream, one based on the aspirations and frustrations of his celebrated Rainbow Coalition. They are no longer where this country is, and he has as much chance of finding support out in the suburbs as he has of being elected chief rabbi in a synagogue.

Nor can the Rainbow look to Bush for relief. Bush thumbed his nose at the people in central cities with his penetrating insight that to solve problems there, "we've got to

---

*For background on the history of Washington's support for Cuba and close ties with the Cuban community in Miami, see Joan Didion's *Miami* (New York: Simon & Schuster, 1987).

teach right from wrong." So we say "amen" to the Great Moralizer and ask for an accounting of his role in the Iran-Contra affair and the crusade against drugs that occurred while he was Vice President. And we ask him to lift his head from his $1,000-a-plate dinner long enough to see beyond all those hogs in the slop buying political favors to notice the real Americans about whom he has given no thought.

By the end of the Smoldering Spring of '92, polls showed that among the major candidates for the presidency a slim majority of Americans felt that Clinton would better serve the cities. The margins were not encouraging, given the fact that Bush had done nothing during his tenure in the White House to suggest he had a clue about what cities need. But the same poll clearly revealed that on the question of law and order Mr. Bush held an overwhelming lead. Unfortunately, city people were not surprised.

It is not just urbanites who are disenchanted. By now most Americans are fed up with the politicians our system keeps coughing up. They know that no candidate deserves support if he or she cannot overcome narrow ideologies of the right and the left in order to give the country more of what it needs. So far no one has come forward who is willing or able to lead the country into its promising future—which is another way of saying that so far no one has come forward who is willing to transcend race and class to give all Americans a promising future. A leaderless nation is ripe for anarchy. Ironically, the word *anarchy* means "without leaders."

Chapter Four

Multiculturalism: When the Country Turns Brown

In Western culture today one must make a distinction between the culture of life and the culture of death (Jules Henry, *Culture Against Man*).

In August 1992 I returned to my hometown in Michigan to attend the forty-fifth reunion of my high school graduating class. I had looked forward to this for months because many of us had begun school together in kindergarten. The East side of town had joined the West side in high school—there being only one high school—and despite our neighborhoods and class differences, we finished together, more or less. Racially the town was white and black, but mostly white. It still looks that way, although there seems to be less reason for blacks to live there than before.

As a boy I came to know rather early on who ran the town and on what side of town they lived. Most of my kind lived on the other side, of course. When I got older, my friends and I, black and white, caddied for those who lived on the good side of town at what seemed to be a well-segregated country club.

Things were simpler then. In our town we all got along,

but we were also aware of life's primary colors: black and white. There were boundaries reflecting distinct values and affecting behavior. We all assumed such distinctions were adhered to universally. Despite the differences, we were the same in many ways. We frowned on those who smoked, and only a few did. Parents stayed married even if the relationship was stormy. Teenagers didn't get pregnant; most rarely if ever got past petting. Teachers taught, students learned—or at least listened—and almost everyone graduated.

Everyone knew what a Chevy was and where it was made. A beard meant either the town was celebrating its centennial or you were Amish. We had never heard the term "ethnic," but we all knew that black people—make that "colored" people— lived in the South. Mexicans were in Mexico, beans in Boston, a bell in Philadelphia, the Democrats in the White House. We also knew that the gods had decreed that all the world should be run by people from Europe and their descendants. If we knew any pop sociology, we called the country a melting pot, never having heard of the Jewish playwright who coined the phrase in salute to this "Republic of Man and the Kingdom of God." We knew that everyone in school was being taught the same values and that we were all expected to melt as we went along. And melt we did, some more than others.

I danced gingerly around my friends at the reunion for fear it would be clear we were at opposite poles of the political spectrum. Los Angeles, still smoldering, is a distant spot from Southern Michigan. But television made it seem right next door. So we played it cool.

In 1992, forty-five years after we graduated, we all knew that the country had changed, though that was not the subject of our conversations. Lee Iacocca's cars now have Mitsubishi engines, Ford owns Jaguar, and the best buy from General Motors is a Saab. How much of a Chevy is American-made is anybody's guess, but by now it is common knowledge that the new direction to look for labor for the industry is South, as in Mexico. Or to the North, as in Canada. Immigrants no longer come in only through the front door.

America has become a pluralistic society, not just in terms of ideas and lifestyle options, nor merely in terms of people with different pigmentation. The so-called browning of America, as a major newsweekly called it, is about different cultures. The popular terms associated with this emerging America are familiar: "minorities," "ethnics," or "multicultural" when used in intellectual circles. What we usually mean by these terms— and what many Americans hear by these terms—is that the place is turning colored. That may not be the case among the academicians or those privileged few who live in the cloistered security of think tanks funded by ideologues of the Left and Right. But to ordinary, everyday Americans, all this talk about multi-ethnicity is about moving over to accommodate more colored people.

The economic implications of this "browning" process for the nation and for those who control it are obvious. As the editor of *U.S. News & World Report* expressed it, "It is sobering to realize that half of the new entrants into our work force in the 1990s will be black, Hispanic or Asian." Just why he sees this as "sobering" is not clear, except that many of these people are ill-equipped to give the leadership necessary to make the U.S. a major player in the high-stakes game of international business. Or he may be sobered by the fact that the nation seems uncommitted to the task of equipping these newcomers to be productive. If that is what he means, he has reason to be sobered. In response, major corporations are getting involved in urban-based public education and special projects to ensure a literate work force for the future. Business spends 30 billion dollars a year in training, but until recently not enough of this has been allocated to areas where the need is most acute. Without such involvement, American business cannot hope to compete in a global economy wherein Japanese young people read and write English better than most of our own kids.

But "our" work force is predominantly white. And to the extent that Hispanics, African-Americans, and Asians break into the work force, they will be working for the most part for white Americans. Black people make up more than 12 percent of America's population, but they own less than 3 percent of its businesses. The reasons range from lack of education, lack of encouragement, and lack of motivation to the unwillingness of banks and loan agencies, including the government Small Business Association, to provide adequate start-up money.

Some are trying to slug their way to the top from the mom-

and-pop stores that dot their communities with the mistaken notion that one day they will arrive at prosperity and security. Someone should tell them that the top is further removed from their grasp than at any time in recent American history. Show me a black athlete who has just negotiated a huge financial package to play games, and I will show you a man whose first act will be to buy his mom and dad a new house and some movin' around space, things they never had before. When white athletes treat their parents after signing the big deal, they have to be a little more creative, because mom and pop already own a nice home.*

These days, even athletes of average ability are assured of landing on easy street. But average white Americans ought to know that the lifestyle they crave and for which they labor is a fantasy, even for the descendants of Beaver Cleaver. The middle-class dream for white America is fast disappearing. So where do all these new people with their non-Western cultures fit? At the back of the bus, unless they are enormously skilled or have managed to bring large sums of money with them. And unless there is a wave of national repentance led by leaders of all political parties, these newly arrived non-Western peoples will likely serve, as black people have historically, as scapegoats for the inability of white people to make it in their own country. I mention all this to make the point that discrimination has little to do with slighting people from other cultures per se. It rears its head only when these people threaten the capacity of the majority culture to make it in society.

The significance of the uprising in Los Angeles at this point in its history is that it happened in a region of America known for its harmonious ethnic relations. Los Angeles once had the reputation of a place to which representatives of the world's peoples decided to come just to prove a point: that all sorts of people from all sorts of places could live together in harmony. Well, more than a hundred languages are spoken in the schools in L.A. You can buy a burrito stuffed with sushi in L.A. One writer has called it "a horizontal city," meaning that,

---

*As Barlett and Steele reveal, "That year [1989], the top four percent of all wage earners in the country collected as much in wages and salaries as the bottom fifty-one percent of the population" (*America: What Went Wrong?* p. xi).

because it has no identifiable central core, it is accessible to the entire basin, thus belonging to everybody. If a Martian were to hover over the city, she would be struck by the amazing variety of peoples within its limits.

The city had had a black mayor for years, and the city council, the seat of real power in the city, had become more representative of the major ethnic groups. So when the 1984 Summer Olympics were held in the City of Angels, the site was almost as important a symbol of global multiculturalism as the event itself. The secular kingdom had not come in all its fullness, but it seemed to be well on its way.

But beneath the surface, the city was in deep trouble. The gangs that seemed to control entire areas, whether Crips or Bloods, threatened to turn huge parts of the city into hostile casbahs. The drug problem had reached epidemic proportions, even if a zillion kilos were being consumed by suburbanites with their own version of a "drive-by shooting." By the mid-eighties, Los Angeles had become one of the drug capitals of North America. Then there were the thousands of homeless people, including children. They were the visible poor, though by no means the majority. The truth is that Los Angeles had become a poor city at its very center. Amid the glitz of its exterior and the success of its athletic teams both collegiate and pro, the inner city down below the famous hillside sign celebrating the glory days of Hollywood had become home for the homeless, the poor, the drug dealers, and the gangs.

So there were—indeed, are—various cultures, ethnic and otherwise, in this city. And they are not always reducible to the nostrums of urban anthropologists. But for all its vaunted multiculturalism, Los Angeles is a segregated city. The areas of ethnicity are carefully delineated and everyone knows their names. East Los Angeles is predominantly Mexican. There are Chinatown and Koreatown. South Central defines huge chunks of ethnic Los Angeles. But these designations do not adequately describe who lives here. South Central is not all black; it is becoming mostly Latino. Baldwin Hills, West Adams, and other "unknown" parts of Los Angeles that are mostly black are nowhere near South Central—and one would get the impression that the pretty faces that report televised news out here didn't know this. These ethnic groups in the city know about each other, but they do not mingle too much. Perhaps they will now.

Koreans know who they are and what they have suffered. They are an embattled people, only recently set free from their own forms of slavery at the hands of imperial Japan. They seem convinced that they are the new "Israel of the Far West," a chosen people. They are a hard-working, hard-driving, no-compromise, get-it-done people. There are 800,000 of them in the United States, up from a mere 10,000 just twenty years ago. They stick together, supporting one another's businesses, borrowing money from their own banks, and buying insurance from their own agencies. They worship in more than five hundred homogeneous churches; 75 percent of all Koreans in the Los Angeles basin claim to be Christians. Only a few Koreans have decided to return to their homeland. The majority have sent a clear message to the city: "We are here to stay; get used to it."

Meanwhile, black people have sent their own message to Koreatown: "If you're going to come over here, make up your minds to join the rest of the city. We are prepared to respect you for your hard work. We are not prepared to put up with your hard-nosed attitudes toward non-Koreans. Your contributions to various causes do not impress us. We have learned long ago that throwing money at the rest of us is not solidarity with us. So make up your mind. Open up or suffer the consequences. If we don't make it, you won't either."

Korean-Americans have begun to get the messages a wounded city has sent them. For all their contributions to the police funds over the years, they still did not have the department's support when they needed it. A top-down culture that has marginalized its own young people cannot hope to participate in the broader politics of a multiethnic city. A Korean church that gives the impression of uncritically baptizing the culture and the ideology of its own chosenness in the interests of church growth cannot hope to guide its young people into mainstream activism.

But a change is in the wind. In the aftermath of the riots, young Korean-American leaders have begun to lead a different kind of march. The kickoff was in Ardmore Park in the mid-Wilshire district, and the date was May 2. The place will become a memorial site and the date a kind of Korean version of Cinco de Mayo. Until the uprising, one had the impression that political activity among Koreans was practiced within the parameters of Korean communities. To be sure, there have been political activists, and Korean-Americans participate in the broader arena of democractic procedures. They vote and they lobby for vested interests like everyone else. But the profile was decidedly low, the tone soft.

The emerging leadership from Koreatown is not only well-trained, but also more experienced in the ways of L.A. politics. There are more women available, and if they can break free from the shackles of an older male-oriented cultural embrace, they will be formidable at every level of city life. Some already are.

The significance of all this is that Koreans are coming of age in America, and Los Angeles is an important landmark in the development of political strategy. What is learned will be "exported" to other cities across the country.

As I listen to the scholarly discussion and debates about culture and multiculturalism, I wonder if those whose education allows them such leisure have driven through town lately. I wonder if colleagues who teach anthropology—cultural or urban—have spent too many of their growing-up years out of the country. The condition of black Americans in our cities is not about changing cultural nomenclature or rediscovering roots; *black* people have been *African, colored, Negro, Afro-American,* and now *African-American.*

Most of the name changes represent the attempts of new generations of black people to come to grips with their real situation, to respond to the psychological burden heaped upon them. Some of the changes have been merely cosmetic, revealing that black leaders have not always been willing or able to confront the cultural realities that shape the values and behaviors of their people. An older generation, observing some of the superficial expressions of cultural change—the wearing of "afros," for instance—argued that what really counts in America is what's *in* your head, not what's *on* it. Speculative analysis by so-called scholars has, more often than not, distracted and prevented society from meeting the problems head-on. Underlying the analysis is the presumption that all black people are the same.

"Latino" people are not one "race" either. And they don't all live in East Los Angeles and drive low-slung Chebbys. Spanish may be a common language in a broadly defined Hispanic community, but there are all sorts of people groups among them who have very little in common beyond ancient suspicions of one another's intentions.

It is well-known that Asian groups are wonderfully different from one another. They typically have no more working or playing acquaintance with other Asian groups than with African-Americans. Like African-Americans, they stay in their own ghettos, venturing out to do business, to attend USC, or to work excruciatingly long hours so that their children can go to Cal-Berkeley.

There is potentially great opportunity to learn from one another in a multicultural society. Unfortunately, the country is experiencing intercultural war. It burst into the public mind with hassles at major universities over the teaching of Western culture and history to the exclusion of other, ethnic under-standings. The debate was fueled by Allan Bloom's book *The Closing of the American Mind* (New York: Simon & Schuster, 1987), a treatise that among other things pleads for a return to classical education. This was followed by a fine piece by noted historian Arthur Schlesinger, Jr., titled *The Disuniting of America* (New York: Norton, 1992), an attack on multiculturalism. Along the way there has been a raft of significant works attempting to explain America's cultural confusion.

But it was Bloom's book that struck a nerve deep in the body of American cultural life. It wasn't just the weight of his argument, which is not always easy to follow. It was the spirit of his polemic that was attractive to many Americans and chilling to many others, especially black Americans. Bloom was clearly angry and out for blood. Apparently there had long been a hunger for someone to come along and put all the events of the sixties and seventies into some cultural and intellectual perspective. Politicians and social scientists had attempted it, but none had worked this field from the perspective of Western cultural thought. Besides, the public, along with many in the intellectual community, had become suspicious of social scientists. Most of them were liberals, and they were the ones who got us into all this mess in the first place. So what *were* all those "flower children" really about back then? And black people in the streets, supported by effete snobs from Manhattan? And Jane Fonda?

The country was past all that in terms of years spent, but not in terms of a need to put all of it into intellectual perspective. Or, put another way, the country was ready for a conservative voice other than a politician's to assure everyone that the policies of the right wing had been right all along.

The response to Bloom's *Closing of the American Mind* went beyond any publisher's dream. It sold more than 800,000 copies, more than enough to ruin the scholarly reputation of almost any professor, at least in the minds of his or her colleagues. Bloom's work was important because it did more than rehash old events. It showed how those events exposed a deeper malaise in Western civilization, and it argued that this malaise raised ultimate questions about the viability of the culture itself.

Bloom was able to touch the nerve because it had been exposed. Something had gone wrong in the society. The trick was to identify it, expose its root system, and if possible find the culprits. The last of these is especially important today. The ability to find the culprit, under the guidance of astute campaign strategists like Kevin Phillips, Lee Atwater, and Newt Gingrich, rendered substantive debates on real issues unnecessary, even self-defeating. Simply identify the people responsible for society's ills, tie a tin can to their tails, and waltz into the White House. When you no longer have the power or the will to fix problems, it is easier to find a scapegoat.

Evangelicals, or at least those few who try to stay in touch with the world of ideas and whose ideology inclines to the right, imbibed Bloom's fare in huge gulps. Many of them quoted Bloom from one hand and the apostle Paul from the other. Bloom became more popular to this crowd in the eighties than Francis Schaeffer had been in the sixties. This was strange in a way, because evangelicals know their history. They know that Enlightenment intellectuals have sought to seduce the Christians in many lands or, failing to do that, have redefined the meaning of life itself, thus making Christian answers to that crucial question irrelevant. One would not gain from Bloom any notion that life's true purpose is to know God and to enjoy God forever.

To Bloom, the meaning of life is knowing oneself, and the goal is autonomy. That, in turn, is what being civilized is about. The key to such a personal enterprise—indeed, to the cultural mandate—is reason. Thus evangelicals' attraction to an intellectual tradition that has systematically shoved the Christian witness from all its major institutions is noteworthy.

There is another explanation for the ready acceptance of Bloom's work among evangelicals. Many sensed intuitively that Bloom's system is basically an argument for the superiority of Western culture and the ideology that exists at its core. If this is indeed the case, it demonstrates further that modern evangelicalism resonates with a critique of recent American culture that supports the basic premises of conservative, fundamentally racist politics. It would further indicate that evangelicals are vulnerable to political seduction, especially from the Right, and that over the past fifty years the evangelical movement has become more American than Christian and over the past dozen years more and more conservative politically.

The marriage of evangelicalism to conservative politics is as understandable as it is strange. It is understandable because for so many years evangelicals served as the theological foils for liberals at every level of American society. They still do for most of the media, print or electronic. With the full-flowering of Billy Graham's influence in the halls of power, however, evangelicals got a foot in the door where influence and power could be expressed, even leveraged. Charles Colson acknowledges this in his interview with Vice President Dan Quayle in the June 1992 issue of *Christianity Today* (pp. 328–31). What impressed me about the interview, apart from the questions Colson could have asked and didn't, was the assertion that not until the Reagan-Bush era did evangelicals have friends in the White House. That is in part why the conservative-evangelical marriage is strange. By any assessment based on sound evangelical theology, Jimmy Carter was more evangelical than either of those good Republicans.

So evangelicals' attraction to the Republican party was based ultimately on political considerations, specifically an agenda dictated by a white majority in the electorate and in the suburbs. As the influence of the evangelical wing has flourished, that of the so-called mainline churches has waned. The latter's leadership has lost touch with the churches and with the culture. Evangelicals have finally come of age—or so it seems. Their representatives are now being summoned to important meetings in the Oval Office whether for the purpose of focusing on the family or addressing the plight of American youth or considering possible alternatives the government might pursue in the Middle East.

Evangelical seminaries have also swelled with an army of young people eager to prove that they, too, can think and have something to say about the direction of the country. In an era in which there is little patience for losers, evangelical churches have experienced steady growth. But for all the prominence and influence, there was very little about modern evangelicalism at the end of the eighties to suggest that it was driven by the desire to apply its theology to the world's systems. The theological debate and discussion continued, although not everyone was invited to contribute. The discussants were all lily-white, even when they were debating Christology—as if Jesus had been born on the hillsides of Georgia or just off the seminary campus in Wenham, Massachusetts.

Evangelicals have become just as involved in worldly affairs as the liberal counterparts they once criticized for doing the same thing. Even evangelism, in some circles, is carried out for the purpose of producing good Americans. In the seventies, while the nation struggled to get its emotions straight over Vietnam and a disgraced President was sent packing to San Clemente, there was a proliferation of flags on evangelical and fundamentalist platforms throughout the country. This was because by the early seventies, conservative believers had become convinced that their best interests lay in marrying themselves off to the emerging mood in the country, a post-Vietnam mood not unlike those mood swings associated with American society after all our wrenching war experiences. Those moods are conservative as long as the country prospers, and this one does. Evangelicals have gotten fat along with the rest of white America, and fat people vote conservative, even if in their conferences they incidentally mention something about justice and mercy.

By virtue of their political involvement, evangelicals—who are mostly white Christians—are caught up in the issues of multiculturalism no less than those people who run colleges and universities or those ethnics who occupy the core of our major cities. Issues of culture cannot be separated from politics. A friend and colleague said something significant shortly after the smoke in Los Angeles had begun to clear. With his usual animation he exclaimed, "Those riots are not about race. It's all about culture. Any of my first-year students could see that." I listened as intently as I could, because he has won the right to make such observations, having spent many years abroad studying cultures not his own. But my initial response was to suspect that he had been out of the country too long, that he was just another missionary with a Ph.D. earned by studying the behaviors of dark peoples abroad. He is more sophisticated than that and so is his discipline, and I suspect he has a lot to teach us in this day when the country is being profoundly affected by people from places other then Europe.

As for his analysis, however, all I can say is that most of us in the black community, or our fellow Americans of any discernible hue, do not perceive that we have experienced discrimination because of our cultural lifestyle. After all, some of us have been culturally white almost as long as we have been anything else. We have paid our dues to the majority culture, as did most of our ancestors, and we, like them, came to see that culture never was the problem. America is still a pigmento-cracy at its core. In fact, the ideology of white supremacy is not sophisticated enough, at the popular level at least, to recognize cultural differences. For many of us, it is enough to walk into a room to know that culture is not at issue. Pigmentation—and the recent experience of numerous white people—is the flip side of the same phenomenon. As a result of the riots, many white people in the Los Angeles basin confess to being aware for the first time that they are white. And for the first time, many of them are afraid—afraid because they are white in a society that is becoming increasingly nonwhite.

The fundamental issue in all this talk about multicultural-ism is power, specifically white male power. If Bloom's book was the shot that triggered a new round of cultural wars, the event that most starkly revealed the reality of the power struggle in America occurred in October 1991, nearly eight months before the riots in Los Angeles. It happened at the other side of the country, in the nation's capital, and most of America watched it on television. What most of us did not see, however, was that this event would alter, perhaps permanently, the balance of political power in the country. Not even evangelicals are safe from being affected by the change. A black man, seeking confirmation for the U.S. Supreme Court, had been confronted by a black woman who had accused him of sexual harassment.

As this face-off proceeded, it became evident that another issue, more deeply ingrained at the core of the American political system than any reference to sex, had emerged. What the nation saw—or at least what millions of American women saw—were the grim faces of white males patronizing a woman as part of their effort to maintain power in high places. Except for their disagreement about certain important facts, Judge Clarence Thomas and Ms. Anita Hill had a great deal in common. They were both black Americans and, despite frequent references by the judge to his humble beginnings in Dixie, culture was a nonissue. Their common bond was that they were both being used by white males trying to retain power in the system.

Based on the mild praise Thomas's record generated from the American Bar Association, it is most likely that had he been white, he would not have been nominated at all. So it seems as if the Republicans believe in affirmative action after all, at least when it leads to political gain. The Democrats, with no courage and very little style, simply abandoned Anita Hill to the wolves. Ted Kennedy's presence on the Senate Judiciary Committee was a joke, of course, given his stellar reputation for indiscreet behavior. The National Association for the Advancement of Colored People was hamstrung, lacking the courage to speak against a fellow black man even though his judicial record showed he clearly stood for the conservative agenda and against those issues most dear to its heart.

The results of the confirmation debacle are not all in, but already a major trend is clearly in view. Clarence Thomas and the white Republicans won the battle, but women may be well on their way to winning the war. By the time elections came around in 1992 the stage had been set for a far-reaching political revolt of sorts among women. In primaries across the nation women won significant support for key offices at the state and national levels. A black woman won the Democratic nomination for a Senate seat in Illinois against Alan Dixon, exclusively—according to all the analysts—because he had voted for Thomas. California, known for its political high jinks, nominated no fewer than sixteen women for the U.S. Congress and two for the U.S. Senate. Women—Asian, black, Hispanic, and white—lined up to challenge the ubiquitous white male for dominance in politics.

It remains to be seen whether white women in power will act more justly than their male counterparts, and it is still distressing that it took a black woman of unusual courage to mount the podium and blow the whistle. It seems that in matters of justice, black Americans still must pay a price to get a movement started.

But if power is the key issue in the struggle toward a multicultural society, it is not always clear what its attainment really secures. Most white males, for instance, unless they hold political office or have scored enormous success in business at top levels, would deny they have any appreciable power. The statistics about divorce and child and spouse abuse at the hands of many of these males would seem to confirm this. Ironically, it is this absence of power among many whites that explains their emotional distress when people of color seem to possess power or are viewed as being positioned to acquire it.

Power becomes the issue in race relations because power is an assumed right on the part of white Americans. "White power" was not a slogan in the country until black people began clamoring for "black power." Until then, white power was simply assumed, both as a right and as a possession. The assumption was the peculiar obsession of white males. As stated previously, this was clearly the issue during the Hill-Thomas spectacle and when white cops pounded on King.

There is a power culture in the society, and this is the reality that confronts people of color in the city. These people know that they are not born to power. This is one question white males do not need to ponder; if they are not born to power, they are the direct beneficiaries of power in the culture. It is the loss of this sense of power entitlement that may prove to be the key to the country's immediate future. In a society where the cultural apparatus seems no longer to support the assumptions of white power, it will be important for the disinherited to find people to blame. If our history tells us anything, the finger of blame gets pointed at the last people off the bus, at the last people hired just before the plant closes, the ones whose work habits caused the decline of product quality— the people who do not share "our" values.

Yet the values of American culture, those trumpeted by the former Vice President, are being questioned throughout the country—and not by the "Murphy Browns" of the society. They are being questioned by the culture's "baby busters," whose objective reality seems not to reflect their subjective commitment to those values. They did work hard, did believe in God, did secure decent grades in school, and did salute the flag every time their leaders called them to arms. They did believe in the ideas of liberty and justice for all. But the ideology has not paid off for the grandchildren of the Baby Boomers, and that makes this crowd a potential powder keg. This is really the generation that will fulfill Saul Alinsky's dark prophecy of an America that moves into either a radical social change or an indigenous American fascism.

From a Christian perspective, it could be argued that such displays of power by white males in secular society are not only illusory, but destructive. Yet any examination of most evangelical Christian organizations reveals the same good ole boy network one finds in that secular society. Interlocking boards of directors are commonplace, and the ancillary perks offered by the wealthy to those in charge of ministries are used to cement these male-bonding relationships. Schools of missions are white-male-dominated even though the work force on the "field" has been predominantly female for years. Women do not seem to enjoy much executive power at headquarters buildings either. Some women were up front at the Manila conference on evangelism in 1989, but they did not function in leadoff spots where theology was articulated. Scarcely does one find a nonwhite faculty member in evangelical circles of higher education, and if one does, he or she is likely to be from a country other than the United States.

Of course there are those who say the absence of African-Americans in leadership positions among evangelical mission-related institutions is due to a lack of qualifications. Presumably, if African-American Christians had prepared as assiduously as their white brothers did, they too would be in places of leadership in missions. They too would have been recognized in Manila—if not on the platform, at least among the faces on the multimedia screens. Surely, in all the years since George Lysle went to Jamaica, to be followed by scores of black believers to mission fields from South Carolina to India, there have been some black missionaries who could have taught something somewhere.

But Manila was, for most of the African-Americans present, the most telling insult to our sense of Christian selfhood in all the years we have ridden in the back of the white evangelical bus. The North American version of the Lausanne movement was widely perceived to be racist to the core, and the unfinished agenda for North American evangelicals was to deal with our own version of Reconstruction. Was this exclusion of black evangelicals at a conference overwhelmingly represented by people from the two-thirds world a mere oversight? A matter of culture? With ample access to supposedly sensitive cultural anthropologists, organizers ought to have known better. Perhaps they did know better. Perhaps there was a concern about power and a related fear that if black evangelicals from North America got themselves together and made some alliances with other men and women of goodwill from other parts of the globe, a new network might emerge, one closer to the ethos of the oppressed than is currently represented by any Euro-American association.

Surely, in all the years Western Christians have labored to spread the Gospel, they ought to have seen the usefulness of African-American persons in missions worldwide and to have invested in them to increase their effectiveness in the interests of the kingdom of God. In a few instances this has happened, but more commonly in the past was heard that tiresome argument about culture. I have heard for years that black Americans could not go to African peoples in the same manner as Euro-Americans. African people have reacted to such thinking with the same puzzlement as black Americans.

The other puzzle in the minds of our brothers abroad has been the behavior of certain missionaries. I was asked about this during lectures in Singapore several years ago, and I had to inquire what my African brother had in mind. He described behavior that could only be called arrogant and racist. "Why," he asked, "have missionaries in my area never invited me into their homes or even to have tea on the front porch—as you call it?" I could only suggest that missionaries who behave like that in Africa do so because they behave like that toward black Americans in their homeland. Most Western missionaries never see a black missionary, nor study with a black missiologist, nor even visit a black congregation before going abroad. People in the two-thirds world have no idea how far apart from each other Christians in this country are and how racism has played such a large role in maintaining this distance.

I have encountered missionaries-in-training and veteran Christians who objected to my line of preaching. They were especially upset that I would insist that the kingdom of God has something to do with justice and that "a theology that does not liberate is no theology at all." When we have engaged in debate over some of this, it has become clear that some of these Christians have never forgiven Martin Luther King, Jr., for dispelling their cozy view of themselves or the value system of their parents. No one to this day has been able to process for them just what happened in those great years when democracy crept up on this country, led by a black Baptist preacher from the Deep South. All some of these saints can tell me, with some heat in the telling, is, "We lived through all that."

If the civil rights movement was not a matter of one culture against another—and I've never heard a missionary anthropologist say it was—then why are current conflicts, including the L.A. uprising, defined as such? If Christian anthropologists can demonstrate that the study of cultural anthropology and its application can put out the fires of tribal warfare in urban America, let us furlough all of them immediately and assign them to First AME Church. If burning a city is not about power and powerlessness, violence and injustice, what does one preach on the Sunday after? What did most preachers in the suburbs preach about the Sunday after the Watts riots in the sixties and the South Central and West Los Angeles riots in the nineties? I know what black preachers talked about. It would make an interesting study to analyze the relationship between a congregation's social standing and sermon topics.

To be sure, no one would deny the presence of cultural differences between black and white Americans. Check out Sunday morning at First Baptist and then swing by Second Baptist Church, and you will be reminded of some of those differences. (By the way, ever notice how many Second Baptist churches are black, and how many First Baptists are white?) But black Americans have been Americans for longer than most white immigrants, and they have rarely wanted to be anything else even when the courts and the government have not always allowed them to reap the full benefits of living in "the land of the free." Only recently, with the Voting Rights Act of 1965, was democracy officially extended to black Americans. That is why it is so painful for black people to watch others get off the plane and get a loan from a bank that won't let a black man get past the front door. And that is also why it is not easy to hear a white brother tell you that the issue is culture, not race.

In sum, brewing in the nation is a full-scale war of people groups against one another, and the issue is power. Powerless groups are beginning to realize that marginality in America is not about being *dumb*—it is about being *denied*. We may have to learn the hard way that powerlessness is the source of violence among any people. Those who have power are not apt to give it away. Thus the only option for a powerless people is to take power away. How it is taken will be decided by those who have power.

Malcolm X made this point in the sixties. He made it known that if white America did not respond to the peaceful, nonviolent message of Dr. King, they would have to deal with his version of "whatever it takes."

Given their life circumstances, it comes as no surprise that a new generation of urban black young people has discovered Malcolm X. And they are not alone. The image that burns itself into my mind is that of a Korean young man brandishing a pistol and wearing a T–shirt covered with Malcolm's words, "By any means necessary." One of my students, a United

Methodist pastor in Los Angeles who is a long way from his teen years, would show up in class wearing a sweater with Malcolm's likeness woven into the fabric. A favorite cap worn by blacks has a simple white X set off against the black fabric. Rappers know about him, and Spike Lee has depicted his career and influence in a new motion picture.

Why Malcolm again? Why now? Does it have something to do with black culture? Malcolm X is a symbol of revolt against oppression. He is only marginally a symbol of African culture either today or during his lifetime. He has come to stand for black manhood at a time when black men, especially black young men, are having a terrible time surviving both psychologically and physically. The current version of the Black Muslims, long associated with Malcolm's memory, shows considerable ability to attract the attention and enlist the allegiance of black youth. Minister Farrakhan speaks too much truth to be totally ignored by anyone. His brashness in dealing with the truth makes him attractive to a broad cross-section of black people in urban centers.

Malcolm X also symbolizes the need for truth-telling between black and white Americans. In circles where black people gather, people respond with knowing approval when someone states that the difference between these two groups is that white people smile at you in public and say all sorts of bad things about you behind your back. Black people would rather have it the other way around: "We are more likely to jam you up front, get it all out in the open. Then afterward we all go for coffee." Or, perhaps Malcolm reminds black young men that they do not have to play the white man's game to be somebody. Black people are black for some important reason; some significant destiny is wrapped up in those ebony bodies. Find out what it is, commit yourselves to it, and forget the Man. Contrary to the Western myth, people of African descent do not exist to make Westerners comfortable; black people were not cursed to be forever the hewers of wood and drawers of water, another myth that many whites (and blacks) can't let go of.

It is not so much a matter of how much Malcolm will influence black youth as of what part of his legacy will be remembered. He could bring white people up short all right, and in that black people rejoiced. But he also became a man of peace and a champion of reconciliation. Not all of us got that message or saw that part of him. I pray that in the urgency of today, we will.

After sifting through the flap over culture and cultures, I come back to Jules Henry. The insight with which I began this chapter was penned in 1965, and over the years, until recently, could have been written with Russia in mind. Presumably we were the culture of life, they the culture of death. To read Henry that way was to have missed the more radical insight that is more readily discerned in 1993. Henry's works are about *all* of Western culture, and his concluding insights are even more provocative:

> Where is the culture of life? The culture of life resides in all those people who, inarticulate, frightened and confused, are wondering 'where will it all end?' Thus the forces of death are confident and organized while the forces of life—the people who long for peace—are, for the most part, scattered, inarticulate, and woolly-minded, overwhelmed by their own impotence. Death struts about the home while life cowers in the corner (*Culture Against Man* [New York: McGraw-Hill, 1965], pp. 475–76).

Chapter Five

Violence American Style

> But the most dramatic evidence of the relationship between educational practices and civil disorder lies in the high incidence of riot participation by ghetto youth who had not completed high school. Our survey of riot cities found that the typical riot participant was a high school dropout (U.S. Riot Commission Report, 1968).

I was relieved when the Los Angeles district attorney's office admitted that its earlier projections about gang membership in L.A. were flawed. The office had originally stated that 150,000 young men belonged to 1,000 gangs throughout the county and that 47 percent of black men between the ages of twenty-one and twenty-four had been recorded on police blotters. Latino gang activity was up, according to the original projection, but black activity was down. The figures were staggering; they immediately drew fire from Latino and African-American leaders. Even the D.A. and the police chief questioned the accuracy of those figures.

So upon finding out there had been a mistake and that the figures would be downgraded, the entire city heaved a collective sigh of relief. Not that we should have, since even the adjusted numbers were not exactly good news. (I don't quote the new figures here, because they may not be any more reliable than the first set.) Regardless of the exact head count, there is no reason to doubt that gang membership is at an all-time high and that violence and murders associated with gangs are still responsible for most of the mayhem in Los Angeles County. Add to this the thousands of children who are growing increasingly insensitive to violence of all kinds and who no longer regard life as significant, let alone sacred, and you have the ingredients for what can fairly be called war.

Unfortunately, gangs do not have a monopoly on violence and death. In 1990, 400,000 American young people between the ages of twelve and nineteen reported having been victims of violent crime (*Newsweek*, 9 March 1991). The image in the public eye is that of black and Hispanic gang members shooting it out over some slice of urban turf. The reality is much broader. Teen violence spreads across demographic and economic lines, often exploding with sudden finality in rural and small-town America and deep into the suburbs. At a toney prep school in Long Beach, California, a small gang of affluent teens was accused of murdering one of its members because he violated one of the codes of their secret clan. (*Clan* is spelled with a "c" in the context of the upper middle class.)

The violence goes far beyond kids shooting kids. It includes parents throwing chairs from the stands or assaulting coaches at a sports event, a motorist shooting at young women driving alone or at the poor guy who cuts him off at the underpass. But it is also the savings-and-loan scam that wipes out the future for thousands economically. And it is junk bonds and international sales of arms that end up in South Africa or in the hands of the nation's enemy in Iraq.

It also includes actions and threats against this country's traditionally disdained minorities. The Southern Poverty Law Center in Montgomery, Alabama, which monitors "hate crimes" in America, notes that the incidence of such crimes among young people has increased nationwide. Blacks and Jews seem to be the favorite targets, judging by the crosses painted on lockers and swastikas scrawled on the walls of synagogues. But black kids and kids from Hispanic back-grounds are having trouble finding each other also. After less than two months into the fall semester of 1992, these kids have exploded in anger and violence toward one another from junior high to high school in L.A.

Despite the persistence of many forms of violence, it is the violence of black youth against one another that seems most to set America's teeth on edge. Today the madness of black-on-black violence is so ubiquitous in urban centers that what was once a stereotype has become a reality. Homicide is now the leading cause of death among black males under the age of thirty-five. Suicide among black males has increased dramatically. The entire country should be haunted by the tragedy of one high school boy who, upon seeing two of his friends murdered at school, went home in hysterics, dialed a friend, and informed him that the click he heard was the sound of a revolver. He was playing Russian roulette, and his friend soon heard the blast that told him the game was over. Marlon Smith was just one of the more than two thousand young people killed by guns between 1970 and 1990.

As I have said, what we are witnessing in our urban centers is the beginning of a real war. Today it is confined largely to young people without direction, many of whom belong to gangs. When they are not aiming at themselves, they are squaring off against the police. They are armed to the teeth, and the arms they carry are not "Saturday night specials." They tote Uzis, .357 magnums, and semi-automatic assault rifles. Even children in grade school feel the need to "carry." They see it as a matter of surviving from day to day. Where do they get these guns? From the homes of the good people they burgle.

Statistics—always problematic—seem to justify the impression most Anglos have about black violence, especially that of black males. If indeed, as one set of statistics argues, one in four black males between the ages of twenty and twenty-nine is either in prison on parole or on probation across the nation, there is cause for alarm. In California a report indicated that the number was even higher: one-third of black males in the state in some contact with the criminal justice system. White males? Only 5.4 percent.

One reason that black males dominate statistics is because more of them get stopped by police than do their white counterparts. Additionally, white kids in the suburbs have

agencies to which they can be referred, safety nets that shield
them from ever going straight downtown. I was confronted by
this reality some years ago while listening to two black cops
overlooking a game of hoops at a local park, and I became
aware of a police dilemma. The brother was a good officer and
as such would bust his own grandmother, or so he said. But he
knew the deck was loaded against black youth. The stereotype
that tends to embrace all black males follows a young man all
the way to the suburbs as he is stopped because of the car he is
driving. The parting explanation after the awkward exchange is
usually, "We had word that a car like yours had been involved
in a robbery."

Yet for all that, crime in urban centers is a reality. Much of
it is committed by black and Latino males, and it is not all
against black and Latino people, as it once was. This juvenile
warfare is one of the main reasons that middle-class people of
all races have moved to the suburbs. The prospect of rearing
children amid all this mayhem has become unthinkable no
matter what one's sociology, race, or politics. Add to this the
deteriorating infrastructure of urban life affecting services,
especially in inner cities, and the trek outward is predictable.
The search is for safety, that ever elusive and increasingly
expensive commodity so vital to upwardly mobile Americans.
To all Americans really, though it can only be realized in any
appreciable degree if one can afford it. For that reason alone it
would be surprising if the suburbs were not nearly all white.

White flight from cities is an old story, of course. It
coincides with economic well-being. But it also coincides with
the government's decisions to aid such movement with available loans. In a revealing piece on a changing America, *Business
Week* chronicled the beginnings of the political process that
developed the suburbs, and, in the aftermath, doomed the
cities to decay. It began with New Deal attempts to get the
economy back in shape after the Great Depression, one result of
which was the gradual overcoming of public reluctance to
accept government aid.

Housing remained in the doldrums until the fifties when,
as the result of the Second World War and the higher birthrate
that preceded it, there was a housing shortage. Uncle Sam
responded with zeal through the Federal Housing Authority.

Loans were attractive for several reasons: they were cheap compared with previous scales determined by the agency, they put a priority on new homes over against remodeling old dwellings, and they demanded that any "inharmonious racial or nationality groups" be excluded. This does not mean that white people who qualified for these loans were racists. It does mean that government policy made it impossible for black people and persons of other nationality groups to qualify. One black person in a block could result in having loans cut off for the entire block.

Government policy also made it easier to move out of a city dwelling into a new home, since the FHA made no provisions for loans for the repair of old structures. The dash to the suburbs was on, and black people were once again left with the weary remains. Government help for these people was not forthcoming, and these areas continued to deteriorate. Black families grew larger, like their white counterparts, except that they had no place to go. Decay was then followed by overcrowding, and frustration followed frustration, culminating in the huge riots of the sixties. Columbia University historian Kenneth T. Jackson argues that "No agency of the U.S. Government has had a more pervasive and powerful impact on the American people over the past half century than the FHA" (*Business Week,* 25 September 1989, p. 95). Black America experienced this influence as another form of violence, a major assault on one's selfhood, indeed one's mental health.

This story can be told in cold statistics, charts, and graphs. It is infinitely more difficult to tell it in human terms. Decaying and dilapidated housing is a kind of urban cancer, a gnawing fungus creeping across the face of blasted dreams. They are viewed in comfort from the freeway, and given enough distance and enough speed, one driving by could swear that those were adequate homes for the area. In places like South Central Los Angeles one could almost think that these neighborhoods, often quiet and lined with palm trees, are more than adequate lower-middle-class communities.

Central city in Los Angeles could be called the Second District. It covers approximately 150 square miles; nearly two million people call it home. It includes more upwardly mobile sections called Baldwin Hills and Ladera Heights and parts of the old movie set called Culver City. Its citizens are black, Latino, and white middle class. Nice mix. But much of the riot footage the nation watched on television was filmed in South Central L.A. because it also includes storied communities named Watts and, henceforth, Koreatown. One could argue that much of the future of the city depends upon what happens in the Second District. The outcome will be determined by how those citizens, along with their elected local officials, businesses, and government at the state and federal levels deal with these various forms of violence.

Jack Kemp understands this. As the Secretary of Housing and Urban Development in the Bush administration, he often sounded like the only Republican who does, and he was one of the few directors in HUD's history to propose a program that breeds hope among the poor and disenfranchised. He too was on a moral crusade, but his was different from Vice President Quayle's. Quayle was willing to tailor his morality to the needs of the party; Kemp seemed unwilling to go that far. Speaking on Cable News Network during the riots in L.A., Kemp revealed that he knew that the Administration's response to the riots was purely political. Bush was parroting the old "law and order" themes of Nixon et al. and ignoring the moral aspects of it. Acknowledging that he, too, was for law and order, Kemp added that "twelve percent of the U.S. population is black. [This population] owns less than a half of a percent of the total wealth of America. Our system has locked in the reward basically for people who have made it and is preventing people who don't have anything but the shirt on their back from getting access to property and the seed corn and the capital and the jobs and the ownership of homes" (quoted in *Gentlemen's Quarterly*, July 1992, p. 154).

Kemp's problem is that the more he speaks of morality, the more he will lean toward the plight of the poor and homeless. His theological motif will become that of justice and reconciliation. He already likes the image of the Good Shepherd, who left the ninety and nine to seek the lost sheep. If Kemp follows that model, he will likely end up on the same stick as did Jesus, because his own party prefers the ninety and nine already in that fold. Or even worse, he will be tagged a liberal. Have mercy! There goes the suburban vote.

It is a fact of life in America that the city-suburban dichotomy symbolizes much of the country's cultural and political warfare. In merely physical terms, the suburbs have come to fulfill the dark prophecy of the Eisenhower Commission Report of the late sixties (an investigation of urban violence separate from the report cited at the beginning of the chapter). The commission, concerned about the growing tensions in the country after the urban unrest of that period, spoke of the possibility that these areas would become "armed camps each against the other." Recall that this report came out in 1969. It sounds like ancient history, like an early sci–fi episode that is now a commonplace and acceptable lifestyle.

Another of the report's conclusions is even more chilling: "Between the safe deteriorating central city on the one hand and the net-work of prosperous areas and sanitized corridors on the other, there will be, not unnaturally, intensifying hatreds and deepening divisions. Violence will increase further and the defensive response of the affluent will become still more elaborate." Fantasy? Consider this: According to the Bureau of Alcohol, Tobacco, and Firearms, there are 66,666,000 handguns, 72,739,000 rifles, and 62,432,000 shotguns in the hands of American citizens. And the weapon most likely to be banned all across the country? The Super Soaker.

Only God knows how much firepower is in the hands of police departments and other paramilitary units across the country. If you are over fifty and white, chances are you have never had cause to worry about how many guns the police possess. If you are over sixty, your image of police may be like Norman Rockwell's: an officer stopping traffic to help a family of ducks cross the boulevard. But police violence, with or without gunfire, cost the city of Los Angeles millions of dollars in lawsuits last year. And if that wasn't enough, a new report issued in July 1992 accused the Los Angeles County Sheriff's Department of excessive force and the cover-up of police brutality. It also criticized the district attorney's office for not following up on the prosecution of violations when offenders were identified by the department. Over a period of six and one-half years, the department referred 382 questionable shootings to the D.A.'s office. That office prosecuted one case.

The report, chaired by Special Counsel James G. Kolts,

reveals a series of nightmarish accounts of brutality and departmental indifference in the face of overwhelming evidence against fellow officers. Kolts, a former judge, and his staff concluded, "This report is a somber and sobering one in terms of the large number of brutal incidents that have been and are still occurring. Within the department there is deeply disturbing evidence of excessive force and lax discipline." In a followup report, the Christopher Commission alleged not only that sixty-two "problem officers," responsible for more than five hundred separate incidents of force and harassment, have managed to escape prosecution, but also that some have been promoted and most are still on the street. Even worse, many of these same officers are now serving as field-training personnel responsible for sharing their street smarts with newer patrol deputies. By any definition, this is violence against county residents aided and abetted by the D.A.'s office.

It is not surprising to read that the commission found significant attitudes of racism expressed by a sheriff's force that is overwhelmingly white. These attitudes were aimed at Latinos, blacks, and Asians especially. Los Angeles County is 40 percent Anglo, 37 percent Latino, 12 percent black, and 11 percent Asian. Yet the sheriff's department is 72.4 percent Anglo. It is also 87.5 percent male. Apart from the issue of racism, the overwhelming male dominance of the department is a source of grave concern among the county's women. Since many of the incidents of excessive force occur during police responses to domestic disturbances, women have come to expect male officers to side with the male abusers more than with female victims. Studies have demonstrated that this is, in fact, true.

In less physical terms, the bifurcation between city and suburbs is a form of psychological warfare. It has profound implications for the education of children and their futures in the economy. Children know this. A Young Life staffer reported on a basketball game between a mostly black team from a city near L.A. and a team made up of white kids from a posh suburban enclave. The game was of no great importance; the score was rather predictable, if not in detail surely in final outcome. White kids don't jump. Until the outcome became clear, the cheering was typical of such teen games: "We've got spirit, yes we do! We've got spirit, how 'bout you!" But, says my informant, when the black team got fifteen points ahead, the chant changed. Now the cheer was, "We've got credit cards, yes we do! We've got credit cards, how 'bout you?"

This ditty profoundly reveals a cultural war between caste groups in American society. This war has been going on for years, but the skirmish begins to turn ugly when the economy gets flat and it becomes clearer that the society is firmly divided between "haves" and "have-nots." White kids in San Marino now know they are not competing with black kids from Monrovia or even other white kids from Arcadia, that formerly safe haven from all that was black and brown. Whites are now competing with the ambitious from Asia, Europe, and the Middle East. Especially Asia: These new kids on the block will put in far more hours studying than the whites will. While their fathers and mothers busily support politicians who offer excuses for American malaise in the form of Japan-bashing— and many of them can be found lolling around the pool munching chips and sipping Dad's booze—these new hyphenated Americans are walking off with the top prizes.

It is still important to live in the suburbs because that is where the better education is. Most of those enclaves have enjoyed de facto private schooling for years. More tax monies are spent on those schools than in the central cities, and where this may not be technically true, the issue becomes moot when one adds up all the other perks that the privileged manage in behalf of their offspring. To be rightly connected is of greater long-range value that being well-educated. Suburban kids know this truth without even thinking about it, and it contributes to their educational lethargy. Why sweat it when your old man is well-connected?

Young people from central cities are not dumb. But most of them do live in a caste system as pervasive as the one out there in the suburbs. Many of these kids have never been in the company of a black or brown businessperson. Conversations around dinner tables at night are not about political issues, deficit spending, which schools are best for which career— Stanford or Wharton? That may be one reason that Broadway Federal Bank was burned during the L.A. riots. The arsonist didn't know it was a black bank. I can hear him say it: "Hey, if we'd've know'd dat, we wouldna burned it." I recall my wonder at discovering that there were black professionals, business people, and teachers in America. I learned that from early issues of *Ebony* magazine. I think I was out of college before I saw a black professor in a classroom. Ancient history? Not really.

Desegregation for inner-city kids has meant very little. Busing children to previously all-white enclaves has solved very little either, although studies have shown that kids improve in learning skills if put in with a mix of more talented people. And there are plenty of those in one's own neighborhood. But busing is not just about education; it is about caste. Poor white kids have the same problem as poor black kids. Put black kids with black kids of considerable talent, and their performance would improve. (See *A Common Destiny: Blacks and American Society*, ed. Gerald D. Jaynes and Robin M. Williams, Jr. [Washington: National Academy Press, 1990], pp. 366–79.) But if this caste culture cannot be broken, there is very little possibility of rescuing this segment of our population from these forms of economic, social, and psychological violence.

I suspect that the ultimate violence in central cities is not physical, but psychological. Our society is in the grip of a pathology of violence. The effects go far beyond the problem of minority women raising babies without fathers. In the suburbs, seemingly well-adjusted families composed of father, mother, and two-and-a-half kids struggle more regularly than we like to think to survive the negative dynamics of their homelife. We are reminded of the grip of violence when we see it tolerated and even glorified on television all the way from cartoons to so-called adult dramas and soap operas.

A report recently issued by the National Education Association reveals another possible contributor to the pathology of violence: schools. By now we are all weary of hearing about the decline of public education. Nevertheless, despite some signs of progress, the educational system is cause for despair. While 33 percent of public school students belong to minority groups, only 12 percent of the teachers come from minority backgrounds: 8 percent black, 3 percent Hispanic, and 1 percent Asian. Furthermore, only 28 percent of teachers are men, the lowest percentage since 1960.

According to Claude M. Steele, 70 percent of all African-Americans at four-year colleges become dropouts (*Atlantic Monthly*, April 1992, p. 68). Steele's article is by far the most enlightening I have read on this topic because he demonstrates that black dropout rates at every level are not due to the usual factors social scientists have cited. They are not, for instance, attributable to economic disadvantages, nor to difficulties encountered in the centuries-long struggle to overcome the effects of slavery, nor to the drug culture in urban neighborhoods. Steele calls the real problem one of stigma: "the endemic devaluation many blacks face in our society and schools." He means by this that black young people feel their presence in school does not influence others in any significant way and makes no claim upon others, especially if those others are white.

Déjà vu. I wrote about the same thing in 1968, discussing the feeling one got then when watching television ads about white cars and black cars. The white cars had the high-powered stuff and of course always finished ahead of the black ones. The NAACP jumped all over advertisers during those years, and the advertisers in turn changed the images. They did not change their mind-set, however.

Now, twenty-five years later, young black people know that while someone looking like them may be in the commercial, the image that really counts—the one that sells the product, that sends the signals to the majority—will still be white. That black face is just window-dressing. We people of color can be thankful to Spike Lee. His breakthrough commercials are the only clue that the real message is not related to the product being sold. The real message is that if you want to have fun, be prosperous, drive fine cars, preside over corporations, fish for bass, or protect your kids by making sure you drive on Michelins, you had better conspire against yourself and be born white. Even when you go to war there is no guarantee you will get the same reception when you get home. Black men and women fought in the desert, but most of the images of returning vets were of whites and their adoring and grateful relatives and friends.

This is what Steele means by devaluation. It is related to the age-old stigma of being invisible as a person precisely because one is visible. Black students in college classrooms continue to report the snubs of professors who ignore their upraised hands, hands that after repeated instances the professors claim they just didn't see. Sometimes the insensitivity to women and minorities is more subtle and passive, as in a seminary setting when faculty argue that Western thought in theological reflection is normative.

The concomitant of devaluation, of course, is powerlessness. And powerlessness breeds violence. If we accept Rollo May's definition of power—"the ability to affect change in one's life or in the life of others"—it is easy to understand why so much frustration exists in relationships in this society. We demand of each other and of our children that we and they make a difference in our world. Yet we refuse to invest in ways to enable the powerless to acquire the power they need to overcome violence and self-destructiveness and to take control of their lives. Perhaps the feeling of powerlessness contributes to the incidence of child abuse and spouse abuse in our society. And could this overwhelming feeling that others ultimately control their lives explain why so many young men among us are ready to explode, waiting for some incident to trigger the blast? Our cities are full of such walking, driving, sitting-next-to-you-at-the-game time bombs.

The irony is that powerlessness transcends race and class and gender. In education there is a basic assumption that informs Americans in general, the assumption that Euro-American culture is superior to all others. And—here is the kicker—that assumption, rather than making white people powerful, has contributed to *their* growing sense of powerlessness. White people, especially those in the great American middle class, had every right to assume that their place in history was secure because of their adherance to these values. When they experience "downward mobility," they have to be profoundly shaken. The gods have failed. As Katherine Newman states in relating this phenomenon to anthropology, "I realized how very damaging the ideology of exceptionalism can be where downward mobility is concerned, for it can lead those who have suffered tremendous disappointment into debilitating self-blame, and it bequeaths to their children a host of anxieties about their own competence and destiny" (*Falling From Grace:*

The Experience of Downward Mobility in the American Middle Class [New York: Free Press, 1988], preface, p. xii).

The antidote for this growing sense of powerlessness among whites is more helpings of the same thing that caused the malady—more doses of the rightness of whiteness. What a burden that must be to have always to be strong, nearly perfect, wise, adequate, brave, clean and reverent, exceptional—all those wonderful Boy Scout traits!

Steele observes that although black scholars and writers have demonstrated for years that America has been made stronger by the meshing of the contributions of blacks with those of whites, one would never gain this impression from the school classroom. "There," says Steele, "blacks have fallen victim to a collective self-deception, a society's allowing itself to assimilate like mad from its constituent groups while representing itself to itself as if the assimilation had never happened, as if progress and good were almost exclusively Western and white" (*Atlantic Monthly,* p. 77).

This is a form of violence to those students. White students need to see that they too are being violated, short-changed, and made vulnerable to those furious frustrations that occur when one's objective experience does not correspond with the accepted cultural ideology. Black students, to find a place where they can find their identity, may well choose a black college. But where do white students go after they have discovered that they still have no real power after all the advantages they inherited? Now do you see what I mean?

Not that a black college guarantees a top-flight education, especially in Mississippi. Even the ultraconservative Supreme Court passed judgment upon Mississippi violence by agreeing that the state had not done enough to bring education in black colleges up to par with their white counterparts. By withholding funds from those colleges, the state had deprived black students of adequate resources in laboratories and other classrooms, necessary equipment for research and writing, and needed repair on buildings and grounds. Once again it was demonstrated that separate did not mean equal.

One way to have resolved that problem, of course, would have been to require white students to attend those black schools in significant numbers. White money would have followed white students. Theoretically whites could have attended these colleges, and that is why for years the state of Mississippi argued that education was on a par for everyone. But white young people are not stupid. They are not about to enroll in schools where education and facilities are inferior. The prevailing mentality is to let black kids have their colleges as long as they are not assured a level of education that will enable them to compete in the marketplace. After all, education is something one can eventually take to the bank.

Mississippi, as the epitome of the Old South, is always easy to pick on. The truth is, its record of educational high jinks to the detriment of black young people is being repeated all over the country.* The Supreme Court's decision on the Mississippi case may help, if it gets enough exposure in the rest of the country. Whoever sits on this conservative court in the future will have at least this one precedent with which to work.

Such help is sorely needed, for it has been well documented that young people of color are not being educated in sufficient numbers and at high-enough levels throughout this country. Major corporations have begun to address this reality. Millions of dollars are being spent by industries and corporations to correct this form of violence. It will be most valuable if the effort can avoid merely turning our young people into slaves of industry, because educating black youth for the sake of the corporation smacks of the same slavery as educating Russian youth for the sake of the State.

Indeed, the arguments for the primacy of education to solve grievous social inequities are problematic. It is clear for instance, that education does not of itself produce character (not even Euro-American-culture-based education, Mr. Bloom). Our most effective thieves are some of the best educated around, and our ethical crisis is the result of an educational system that worships at the shrine of relativism. Not only that, but if education can support the machinery of industry and

---

*For an update on this trend, see the report on the current flap over the $112 million renovation project going on at Tennessee State University in Nashville. Black students claim that the only reason such sums are now available for their long-neglected campus is that by 1993 the school is required by law to become 50 percent white.

production, the larger questions about the purposes of life are still left unanswered.

Ironically, Russia, Korea and Japan are perfect examples of educational systems which, though based on different ideologies, have produced a similar crisis of values. "After the collapse of our whole system, who are we?" a Russian might well ask. A Korean or Japanese, basking in abundance and in danger of getting even more prosperous, might well ask the same question, "After prosperity, who are we?"

It is becoming clear that America will pay a dear price for this psycho-technological approach to education, especially where its underprivileged citizens are concerned. For one thing, these people, as they come of age, will not participate in the democratic process. They will have compelling reasons not to, the most glaring of which will be that they have no energy left for ideas after the daily struggle to survive. For another, they will have concluded that the very process they are called upon to support is set against them. This is the legacy of politics for the privileged—a country of, by, and for people who can afford a Political Action Committee.

Americans who are struggling to define the purposes of a democratic system seem afraid to raise the purpose questions lest they offend those more interested in being politically correct than in returning to fundamentals. In the absence of this set of questions, education becomes merely utilitarian, and workers, even at top levels, exist for either their own comfort or for the whims of the military-industrial complex. Saving people is much harder than building a new research center to build more Chryslers.

An older America, with perhaps a greater commitment to its children than appears to be the case today, thought of education as being related to character, not productivity. In our era, character is a lost value in no small measure because morality and ethics have been expunged from our educational enterprise. Herein lies the ultimate betrayal of our children; herein lies the greatest violence of our time.

Chapter Six

Evangelicals and the Urban Crisis

In 1967, these necessities were largely provided through the prompt and laudable actions of local and state government agencies and of private organizations, including churches and neighborhood groups (U.S. Riot Commission Report, 1968).

There is a sense in which the phrase "evangelicals in the city" is an oxymoron, a contradiction in terms. Evangelicals, the old variety at least, have not been in the cities for years in any significant strength. Even the Church of the Open Door, that bulwark of the faith that had anchored one branch of evangelicalism for so many years, finally escaped Los Angeles a few years ago. Free at last! The same scenario has been played out in most cities throughout the country. Even if the old building is still in use, most of the members commute to the Sunday meetings, some from as much as a hundred miles away.

Evangelicals have been fleeing cities since the late eighteenth and early nineteenth centuries. The reasons for their exodus then are strikingly similar to those advanced today. Departing was considered more conducive to godly living, and one could be spared the "dangers, cruelties, bad language,

suffering and immorality that filled the crowded . . . streets"
(Robert Fishman, *Bourgeois Utopias: The Rise and Fall of Suburbia*
[New York: Basic Books, 1989], p. 58). Those streets were in
London, and evangelicals there—among them the famed
William Wilberforce—relocated beyond this threat to the village
of Clapham, five miles distant. They became known as the
Clapham Sect and, assured that their women and children were
safe, were at last free to pursue their notions of solid family life,
all the while filling their evangelical lungs with fresh air. And
who then would be responsible for the lost souls of the dirty
cities? The Salvation Army?

Yet a closer look at American cities reveals a significant
evangelical presence. There are hundreds of churches and
parachurch ministries there, involving thousands of people.
They come in all sizes and with varying degrees of expertise
and effectiveness. Most of them find themselves being over-
whelmed by the waves of new and different immigrants and
the complexities of urban living, but their energy levels are
amazingly high and their presence appears to be the city's only
real hope.

Politicians do not like to recognize the urban church except
during election season. Every two to four years they drop by on
a Sunday or appear for a few minutes when a ministerial
alliance is in session. Everyone knows how the game is played,
and most preachers play along. It breaks the monotony of some
of these meetings.

The attitude of these politicians changes in the off-season.
Maybe the reason is that they just get concerned about church-
and-state issues. More probably, it is that politicians are, for the
most part, secularists. When they talk about the city, they do
not usually tout its churches. They prefer to rhapsodize about
its business opportunities, its universities, and its sprawling
boulevards that run between impressive buildings in which are
stored huge libraries or the artistic expressions of a culture.
Churches are valued, but not in any sense crucial to the life of
cities. That is why the city of Los Angeles omitted any reference
to the churches or synagogues in its premier public relations
piece heralding the city's bright future. In the celebrated U.S.
Riot ("Kerner") Commission Report, there is one mention of
the churches—cited at the head of this chapter—and the report

covers two years of research and nearly six hundred pages in the paperback edition. Secularists make no room for any outside interference in their assessments or planning—until there is a riot.

What the country witnessed during the Los Angeles riots of 1992 was a battery of politicians and business leaders pounding on the doors of key churches in the inner city. They didn't visit libraries or attend concerts. They knew that if there was any possibility of restoring a semblance of order, it would not, in the long run, lie in the hands of the police or the national guard. Nor would it be accomplished by the good ole boys in the state capital. The churches would have to do it, just as they have been trying to do it without a whole lot of help for many years. Waging peace is the church's calling, and those whose political decisions make it difficult for citizens to live peaceably find their way to these churches only when war breaks out.

One such church is First African Methodist Episcopal on the city's near West Side. There are others, of course: Trinity Baptist Church, which is celebrating its seventy-fifth year in the city; Holman Avenue United Methodist Church, whose fine pastor, James Lawson, is a veteran civic leader; and Mount Zion Missionary Baptist Church, where the venerable and ever-popular E. V. Hill presides. It is as the novelist Walker Percy put it when surveying the churches in a mythical Southern town: "some on the Right, some on the Left."

Historic First African Methodist Episcopal Church, founded in 1872, has become one of the mega-churches in Los Angeles. With a membership of nearly eight thousand, it has become one of the "in" places to be on Sunday mornings. The church boasts one of the most accomplished and exciting choirs in America, and its pastor, Dr. Cecil Murray, sees to it that music and preaching are in abundance and served up hot. A great mural depicting the pilgrimage of African-Americans from Africa to present-day America dominates the front of the the impressive sanctuary, signaling respect to the faith of the fathers and mothers of the culture. The conspicuous display of fancy cars outside and of visiting celebrities inside notwithstanding, the church has recalled its African roots and, like many black churches across the country, has spearheaded a renaissance of black history and culture in the grassroots of the community.

This congregation, like many other AME churches, derives its tradition and much of its theology from Methodism. But it expresses its ethos in a more African and charismatic style. Black churches, no less than the growing churches in other ethnic communities, sound and feel like quasi-Pentecostal congregations. The truth is, they are learning to identify with the deep hurts of the black communities in which they reside. Even those blacks who commute are finding ways to make a difference. On visiting First AME, I was impressed with the way the men are giving new meaning to that old European marquee *BMW*: Black Men Working. Older men are fashioning new relationships with black youth and young men, serving them as mentors, and equipping them to find work and advancement in the city.

A ride down the avenues and streets of Central Los Angeles reveals hundreds of churches: stately buildings, store fronts, denominational centers, and other, independent expressions of the faith. Some of these churches are well-known throughout the area and in the networks of people among whom they labor. All of them have unique, historic identities, and some are busily engaged in either fleshing out these identities or trying to get past them. Many of them are in transition, their older leadership having died or having been replaced by younger men—and a few women. Very few.

These churches have at least two things in common: They are nearly all evangelical in their understandings of orthodoxy, and they are in the city, urban to the core. Of course, their understanding of evangelical faith is not shaped by references to the Institute at Wheaton, let alone places like Montreat, North Carolina, or Pasadena, California, or even Wenham, Massachusetts. Their doctrinal traditions were set before the Civil War; they express the basic tenets of the Reformation and the revivalist heritage of the Wesleys or that other revolution that began over on Asuza Street. Not all of these churches have seminary-trained pastors by any means, but that does not concern them.

Seminary-trained pastors or not, the congregations are unfailingly committed to the Bible as the Word of God and to the conviction that salvation comes through Jesus Christ alone. Moral values stem from the same biblical source that is claimed by other evangelicals across the land. Any scholar wishing to verify the evangelical roots of these churches would need only to check the minutes of old denominational and mission committee meetings. They have always believed strongly in prayer, Bible study, evangelism, and missions.

If one's journey across the face of the city included East L.A., the Protestant presence there would express the same evangelical root system. Ofttimes this runs parallel to the basic tenets of the Roman Catholic tradition with which many of these Hispanic church members originally associated. The virgin birth, Christ's substitutionary atonement, the authoritative Scriptures as the only rule of faith and practice—all the basic stuff of evangelicalism is there, whatever the official denominational affiliation. In Koreatown, church members are as evangelical as one can get, even if their allegiance seems to be tilted toward denominational centers in Louisville and Nashville. The real tilt is still toward Seoul, and that means an evangelicalism that asserts not only a firm belief in the Scriptures, but a fervent passion to see churches planted all over the face of the world. The Korean Church is a militant church, surging with energy and committed to worldwide evangelization. It does, however, share something with its North American white brethren: Social justice is not much in evidence on its agenda. Yet.

What I have briefly described in the City of Angels is by and large true for every major city in America. The Protestant presence in other cities, as in L.A., is mostly nonwhite and essentially evangelical in its theology. Yet it is not the standard-brand, evangelical subculture to which whites are accustomed. And so these churches may seem foreign to white brethren from the suburbs. Urban congregations have come to their own conclusions about how the Gospel should be preached, how ministry should be defined, and what shape the primary values should take as derived from biblically grounded theological ethics.

Suburban churches that have any contact with the city will continue to critique the viability of the urban churches' definitions of ministry there. But black Christians find it difficult to listen. They know that white churches opted out of the city years ago, thus forfeiting the right to define anything for them. They also know that while the white church, especially its evangelical wing, is often critical of urban churches' attempts to contextualize the Gospel, there is no better example of questionable contextualization than the experience of that very suburban church. By and large, the contemporary suburban church is "market driven." Some black leaders would even label the suburban Christian reality syncretistic. Truly, it is sometimes hard to tell where the evangelical church leaves off and secular American culture begins.

The division between urban and suburban expressions of Christian faith reflects almost exactly the differences between secular Americans in the city and those in the suburbs. America is today clearly divided—politically, economically, culturally, racially, and religiously—between the suburbs and the city. Generally, Republicans live in the suburbs, Democrats in the city. There is prosperity in the suburbs, poverty in the city. Civic and business leaders reside in the suburbs, and marginalized human beings try to survive in the city. In the suburbs there is contentment with the status quo; in the city there is ferment for social change. In suburban pulpits are found genteel charismatic pastors whose preaching is tinged with yearnings of self-fulfillment. Their urban counterparts are fiery, foot-stomping, change-agent, Bapti-costal preachers.

The positions and strategies of politicians will, more and more, revolve around these realities as they attempt to take advantage of the fears, frustrations, hopes, and aspirations of their constituencies. Thus, in the campaign of '92, George Bush spoke about the needs of the poor in the cities and decried the despair expressed in violent behavior. But his appeal to those he counted on to keep him in office was to law and order and to the nonnegotiable right of Americans to feel safe in their homes and on the streets. Bill Clinton's challenge was to address these same concerns about safety without totally forsaking any remaining vestiges of the old liberal social agenda.

Safety has become the new god of the suburban multitudes. Their heads are full of scenes of urban violence and of stereotypes of bad education in schools where even elementary-age children are not safe. These images are supplied by television and reinforced by print media. Add to all this the threat posed by overcrowded freeways, smog, and polluted water, and the stampede to green grass and Jacuzzis is inevitable. This passion for safety has made a mint for suburban developers, who are selling safety—or its illusion—like the proverbial hotcakes. Gated communities dot the landscape everywhere, and sophisticated, coded card-entry systems are as ubiquitous as American Express, even in the most ordinary-looking condo villages.

Other developers have preferred the walled-city approach. As the desert blossoms like a housing development in Simi Valley, countryside and hillside have been turned into one fresh-looking community after another. From these new com-munities—and that is what they are invariably called even if those who live there have no idea what it means to live in community—former city dwellers now commute to work, even if work is two hours away one way. The air is fresher out there, of course. And there are fewer of "them." As these compounds have multiplied, so has the need for security. So up go the walls, sometimes surrounding the entire complex. All that is lacking in some places are turrets on the corners with armed watchmen. For their sake, I hope the security systems are working. It would be a shame to pay out all that money and end up with just another prison with fancy walls.

People in the cities are concerned about safety, too. Mothers who sit in their living rooms trying to encourage their kids to finish their homework are concerned about safety. That is why some of them have pistols in their laps. Men, newly released from servitude at a General Motors plant that has just closed, are as deeply concerned about the safety of their sons as any father who dials his wife from the front seat of his safety-first Volvo on his way home from the office. The difference is that people in the cities don't have as many options to take safety precautions. And they are running out of reasons to feel secure. Their hopes and expectations are in decline. They have become aware that the drift of the political winds is away from them. They are the ones who are now feeling isolated and adrift in some of the same ways white, working-class Americans felt during all those years when the cities were center stage and the

liberals were in charge of everything. City people feel abandoned and betrayed.

This sense of abandonment is reenforced by the rhetoric of
recent political campaigns. The Democrats appealed to this
sense of alienation by promising a slicker, revised version of the
New Deal. But to win they had to convince suburbanites that
they really didn't mean what they said an hour ago downtown.
The Republicans didn't have to bother with changing their
speeches—they conceded the cities to the Democrats years ago.
The Republicans have known for a long time that the votes are
in the suburbs. The money is there, too. The election of 1992
was the first in the nation's history in which a majority of the
votes cast were by people living in the suburbs. For many of
those voters, it was payback time. At this writing, it is too early
to assess the significance of this voting bloc to the Democratic
win.

The country for years to come will be divided between the
suburbs and the city. The divisions will not be based merely
upon geography. They will be about values, ranging from
definitions of a "normal family" to abortion to taxes to lifestyle
options. Not only will the debate shape political positions and
platforms, but it will solicit the participation of religious leaders
as well. For as Gary Wills has demonstrated in *Under God:
Religion and American Politics* (New York: Simon & Schuster,
1990), religion and politics have run side by side throughout
this nation's history. They act upon one another. In their rise to
power, liberals were able to count on left-leaning mainline
church leaders to assist them in shaping a national consensus
on everything from civil rights to abortion.

With the coming to power of conservatives, there was a
shift away from the mainline churches—which had been losing
members   anyway—to   more   conservative,   right-leaning
churches and movements. The issues that surfaced were not
those associated with life on the city's mean streets. They were
issues connected with upward mobility and the comfort of the
white middle class that is now inhabiting the suburbs. These
conservative church groups performed quite well for their new
masters, even though they didn't get everything they wanted.
The lines of ideological and theological division between the

church in the suburbs and the church in the city were clearly drawn.

These tensions are being lived out among evangelicals no less than among devotees of so-called mainline churches. What is known as the evangelical movement has become essentially suburban in character. The trend was established even before *Christianity Today* moved its editorial offices from Washington, D.C., to Wheaton, Illinois. That move signaled an important change in the magazine, a change more cultural than theological. Today it ought to be called *Suburban Christianity Today*. Its board of directors comes from suburbia, as do most of its writers, most of its editors, and all of its management elite. Not surprisingly, this is reflected in the values espoused in the magazine. Moreover, this holds true for every other evangelical publication and publishing house, with the exception of *Sojourners* and *The Other Side*, neither of which is usually associated in the public mind as mainstream evangelical. In fact, they don't consider themselves mainstream evangelical. One reason for this is that they have remained in the city.

This reality is not necessarily a bad thing. But it does make one wonder how a certain evangelical enterprise can go on professing to represent "Christianity today." Of course, it is easy to pick on *CT*. Any organization that has done something as well as *CT*—and prospered doing it—is bound to draw a lot of fire. Os Guinness, the accepted and acceptable evangelical culture critic, took a shot at *CT*'s sister magazine, *Leadership*, accusing it of not grounding its understandings of the church's mission in theology. But I have not read any criticism that Christianity Today, Inc. publications represent middle- to upper-middle-class white suburban Republican culture.

Several years ago, while I was spending a sabbatical leave in Wheaton, I stopped at the *Christianity Today* offices to see some of my old cronies from Youth for Christ days. Some of them run the place, and I have loved them for years. I was asked what I was up to and what I would like to do as I inched toward my retirement years. I replied as best I knew, and then decided to have some fun. "As to what I'd like to do," I said, "I'd like to write a counterpoint column to Chuck Colson's on the back page of your magazine." Silence. Then weak smiles all around. They knew and I knew it wasn't going to happen.

Everywhere one looks, modern evangelicalism is becoming increasingly elitist. This is evident at evangelical colleges, at conferences, at publishing houses, at all the institutions responsible for creating a sense of rightness in the movement. Key leaders at some of our evangelical college and seminary campuses have expressed a growing concern that Christian higher education is forever out of reach to lower-class young people, regardless of ethnic background. This elitism is innocent, to be sure. Majority white students do not like to think of themselves as being above others. They are elitist, not in spirit, but by virtue of being born into privilege and the ability to afford a first-class education.

Many young whites, along with the few nonwhite young people on these campuses, are having a hard time coming to grips with the pervasive ethos on campus. Resident nonwhite faculty are hard to find. Speakers at chapel and special events are uniformly Anglo. No one is going to tell these few nonwhite students why some of us from "that seminary in Pasadena" are not invited to their schools. (White leaders have assumed all along that black people who are overtly evangelical are impressed with their internecine wars about the Bible, evangelism, and missions. For the record, we aren't and never were. Most black students at evangelical colleges today were not yet born or were barely this side of kindergarten when the "battle for the Bible" and various other causes heated up. They know little about Billy Graham and have never even heard of Harold Lindsell. Those of us who do know these and other combatants saw those skirmishes as more political than theological in nature. The true struggle was over who would control the evangelical club. Had it been more than that, I suspect it would been called something other than a battle. And the debate would certainly have been carried on in a more collegial manner and with a more decidedly Christian spirit.)

The suburban captivity of mainline and evangelical churches—along with their major representative institutions—was one reason that leaders in the mainstream black denominations as well as many black evangelical leaders were attracted to the motif of liberation when it first surfaced in the late sixties. If the theology of white institutions was not inadequate in itself, the argument went, it was rendered so by its adherents' refusal to apply it. Among black Christians, James Cone had lit fires of his own by asserting that black power was the central message of a church true to the Gospel of Jesus Christ. This triggered heated debates in theological circles and among major gatherings of national church bodies. Men such as Cone and Martin Luther King, Jr., had made black evangelicals question their long flirtation with mainline evangelical institutions, institutions that seemed unwilling to acknowledge the problems and feelings of black brothers and sisters.

Rifts that occurred among black church leaders at that time were part of a shaking of the foundations across the theological spectrum. Theologians from the South joined their voices to Gustavo Gutierrez', and others added their efforts to rescue theology from the palsied grip of Euro-American scholars and churchmen. A new generation of writers emerged from all this. When they could not find publishers for their insights among establishment houses, they made their way to Paulist Press and Orbis Books, which became the official outlet for disenfranchised theologies and their creators. (The mere mentioning of Orbis Press in some evangelical circles is considered obscene.)

The issues then—and those dividing believers today—were and are deep-seated. They go beyond merely reaching different theological conclusions: The divisions represent different hermeneutic starting points. Simply put, the Bible is understood one way in the barrio and quite another in the comforts of suburbia. People approach the text with different eyes: One's point of view is determined largely by one's point of viewing. Noted Lutheran theologian Carl Braaten claims that the world is divided between people striving for meaning on the one hand and people living in misery on the other. This is but another way of dividing the world between the "haves" and "have-nots."

It should be acknowledged that poor people struggle for meaning just as much as those accustomed to wealth. And wealthy people are often more miserable than their poorer counterparts. Poor people do not have opportunities to sit on a psychiatrist's couch or have access to lavish churches where pastors expound theologies of self-fulfillment. But in their fragile communities they often experience profound expressions of love not found among the country-club set.

Yet, when there is an absence of meaning among the poor, deprivation becomes hellish. Meaninglessness is the fire that lights up every corner of Hades. Engulfed in this terrible spoilage, people dive into bottles, drugs, and all sorts of incoherent violence, including that most monstrous condition called apathy. Without meaning, there is no hope. And hopeless people shrivel up like raisins in the sun. They may never explode, Sister Lorraine, but if they do, it will be because they knew they had nothing to lose.

The evangelical church in the suburbs has virtually no comprehension of the hopelessness that abounds in this needy mission field just a couple of dozen miles away. Nevertheless, it sees itself as called to proclaim the Gospel to all people and to translate the values of the Judeo-Christian heritage into all levels of the culture. This has been done in all sorts of ways historically, from revival meetings and citywide crusades to—lately—luncheons at the White House. It has not been done in the city—not recently, anyway.

Many evangelicals' vision of a just society borrows heavily from both the sacred text and the best of Enlightenment thought. They do not all know about the latter association, but they suspect its civil-religion truth as they lustily sing the national anthem before their local team plays ball. This analysis does not apply to all evangelicals. But even some of my Mennonite friends have gotten so cozy with the culture as to give Menno Simons fits were he with us today.

The evangelical church in the city is less concerned about its formal orthodoxy or how that relates to the broader American culture. Instead, it is more interested in translating its understanding of the Gospel into forms that can be recognized by the oppressed as "good news." Thus the hermeneutic base is different. The very starting point from which questions are raised and priorities determined is as different as the "haves" are from the "have-nots."

As cities take on a more non-Western ambiance, replete with substantial unemployment and political disenfranchisement, urban and suburban churches will be further distanced from one another along faultlines of ideology and praxis. The church as a whole will continue to live with the bifurcation between evangelism on the one hand and social responsibility

on the other; between justice on the one hand and reconciliation on the other; between an ecclesiology defined along
dispensational lines and an ecclesiology defined more in terms
of the reign of God on earth.

Ultimately, the church in the city will have to go it alone.
This has been apparent for years. Leading urban pastors have
long given up any real hope that things could be different.
Their churches have been indigenous and self-supporting as
long as anyone can remember. Talk about cooperation between
urban and suburban churches has, for the most part, been just
that—talk—even though the very future of the city itself is at
stake. Lerone Bennett was correct in the sixties when he
claimed that the issues infecting cities were not about black
people and white people per se, but about cities themselves and
about whether democracy could survive there (*The Negro Mood*
[Chicago: Johnson Publishing, 1964]).*

I have shared that view for years. All the pent-up anger in
the streets, the hollow-eyed visages of single mothers trying to
keep their children, boys and girls rummaging through urban
litter for lack of something to do or to find something to eat—
all these are ultimately about democracy in America. Given
their present status, these people cannot participate in the
system. It is not hard to understand why they feel no obligation
to attend to its well-being or to obey its laws. The open question
after all these years of social management and experimentation
is whether democracy will return to the city—or whether it can
without help from the suburbs.

As of now, it appears the suburbs are not of a mind to
entertain the question. Forty-five percent of Americans now
live in the suburbs. Nearly 40 percent of the work force
commutes from suburb to suburb because manufacturing and
related industries have moved there. Nearly 60 percent of all
the office space in the country is located in the suburbs. Urban
churches can read the graffiti on the freeways. It is called
advertising, and it is not aimed at the central cities.

---

*In addition to talk, there have been significant "love-ins" and prayer rallies
in major centers. These are led by such luminaries as Lloyd Ogilvie, pastor of
Hollywood First Presbyterian Church; Jack Hayford, pastor of the Church on
the Way; and Fred Price, pastor of Crenshaw Christian Center.

If the city has any hope, it lies with the church. It is not that the future of the city depends solely on the church, but rather the glue that holds so much of the city together, certainly in black communities, is the church. Here the city's political leaders come for nourishment. Here its teachers, musicians, scholars, and families find inspiration and hope. The urban church is the hub of the community in ways foreign to its suburban counterpart. For this reason, the urban church carries a burden not required of its wealthier brothers and sisters elsewhere.

There are occasions when help from the suburbs is available, especially in potentially explosive or desperate situations. But over the long haul these churches will have to build alone upon their own foundations, extending their own borders from within. This will not be easy. Many of the pastors in the central cities are aging. Likewise, the black church, long the bulwark of central cities, is an aging church. Many of its brightest young adults have departed to glitzier independent congregations, there to pursue a confirming word for a black version of Yuppie living. Some left also because they felt that the educational levels of older pastors left them unable to fill the void created by their new, more sophisticated needs.

These Buppies could no longer be sustained by the same ole grits and gravy Sunday after Sunday. Any conversation with these talented young adults reveals that they needed a place where their gifts and talents could be employed. In churches where traditionally the pastor is king and where "God only speaks to one person in this church," the ministry of the laity is seriously underdeveloped. The cry is for new styles of leadership, less authoritative and hierarchical and more collegial and participatory. As Max De Pree puts it, these churches need to become "Jazzy." Otherwise, their future viability is in question.

Much of the leadership in urban churches is undertrained. Although many of these pastors have managed to do quite well without formal theological education, their young people are now getting degrees, attending workshops and seminars, and asking better questions than their elders could. Significantly, the most influential churches in urban settings across the nation are being led by well-trained, well-educated younger pastors. I suspect that these pastors are in many ways more at home in the city than were previous generations of leaders. For though the black church is an urban body, it has a rural, Southern soul. Thus the annual revival meeting in the older tradition is often preached by someone from the South, usually from the area from which the founding pastor or most of the early members came. The sights and sounds of those meetings as well as of the usual Sunday style are an extension of those rural rituals. So is the meal afterward.

In contrast, the newer leaders may have relatives in the South, but their feet are more at home on asphalt than in red clay. They are products of the city; they know its rhythm and beat. Yet they have not forgotten the importance of their Southern heritage, so on Sunday mornings can be heard a blending of two traditions in the music and preaching. But the black church of the next century will be a totally urban enterprise in ethos and definition. It will require a well-trained and very sophisticated leadership. Whence this training will come is a question that ought to challenge theological centers across the land, and especially evangelical seminaries because of their more focused emphasis on evangelism.

Forces external to the local congregation will severely strain even the most able leaders. Family life as traditionally experienced is all but gone in most communities. The values still exist, even among the young, but the role models have disappeared. In addition, economic incentives militate against the values of the church. Young people can find few or no reasons to stay in school, while thousands of them find the pressure to conform to gang life overwhelming. Indeed, this is a frontier of ministry for which very few pastors and youth leaders are equipped.

Another reality the urban church must confront is the oft-noted precarious future of the black male. For scholars and analysts, this topic has been reduced to sociological jargon. For a black man in the city, this is an embarrassing, deeply felt, and painful reality. His vulnerability is due in large measure to a lack of education for the kind of economic world that no longer needs what he might have to offer. Alvin and Heidi Toffler argue that most of the ills of an urban world are, at root, economic: "The new racism and the new unemployment spring from a new system of wealth creation that is spreading swiftly through all the affluent nations, destroying the 'mass society' of the industrial past."

The Tofflers' explication of this new "de-massified" economic system, this Third Wave of change, is well worth considering. According to the argument, today's young people are being "educated" for an economic system that no longer exists. Citing a listing of the top one hundred companies in California published by the *Los Angeles Times* just before the Rodney King verdict and the ensuing riots, the Tofflers observed that there was "not a steel company or an automaker among them. Not a textile mill or a cement company. The key companies in the economy inhabited by Rodney King and ghetto young people . . . are in fields like pharmaceuticals . . . computer software . . . medical insurance . . . semiconductors . . . management consulting."

The same would probably be true if the scene were shifted to Boston. Though I wonder, Do they still make rifles in Springfield? Pistols in New Haven? I know they sell a lot of cocaine there, just a few blocks from Yale University, in fact.

Indeed, the challenge facing Peter Ueberroth and his coalition, whose task is to rebuild Los Angeles, is not an enviable one. I hope they are reading the minutes of all the efforts expended to rebuild Detroit after the riots of the late sixties. It was called "New Detroit," and it seems to have ended up in Troy, Southfield, and Auburn Hills. The coalition might want to heed the Tofflers' parting shot about the new economy:

> There can be no permanent peace in the black and Latino ghettos of America, the North African banlieues of France, and the barrios and immigrant slums of the rest of the high-tech world until all industrial-style institutions, from health systems and justice systems and, yes, political systems, are redesigned for a Third Wave society congruent with the new Third Wave system for creating wealth (*World Monitor*, 18 June 1992, pp. 16–18).

Amid their similarities and differences, urban churches share a heritage rooted in the Third World. This heritage includes the African-American church despite its long history here. Generally these congregations have strong communal ties. They have learned to care about people, to nurse the stranger, to find room for one more. They know that for them there has been no hidin' place down here, so they create shelters for one another. They know—at least the African-Americans know—that people of color usually have common enemies. Because of this, they ought to have a compelling interest in supporting one another.

It is not that simple, of course, for there is too much cussedness in all of us to support others as we should. As I have said, the unity found in the common struggle is balanced by disunity generated by competition for what little remains of the American pie. Suffice it to say, there are some important starting points for unity among a newly emerging collection of churches in the city.

The new evangelical church emerging in urban America will have an unprecedented character all its own. Short of major reversals in the national political and economic agenda affecting urban centers, it will increasinlgy become for the most part a church for the dispossessed, for those whose lives are lived at the margins of society. The upwardly mobile will drive by on clogged freeways wondering what is happening in the old place. Or, fearful of getting shot at from the hills above, they will simply stay away, safe in their Clapham villages.

Chapter Seven

Where Do We Go From Here?

Can we all get along? Can we stop making it horrible for the older people and the kids? [Rioting] is just not right. It's not going to change anything. We'll all get our justice (Rodney King).

I have been a fan of Lee Trevino's for many years. For Americans who watch golf and celebrate a land of equal opportunity, Trevino is Exhibit A. So when he smiles at us from the front seat of a Cadillac and asks, "Is this a great country or what?" we grin knowingly and are once again reassured, especially those of us who used to caddy at the rich man's clubs. We know you can scarcely do that anymore, what with the advent of the electric cart. Mexican and black kids are not going to get into golf by the caddy route these days, nor into fine colleges with caddy scholarships. White kids will, though. There is plenty of scholarship money floating around at the wealthy clubs. So we cherish Lee Trevino. He is likely to be the last of his breed.

It is a long, hard way from the back end of a Cadillac where Trevino used to load clubs for the rich folks to the front seat and lucrative contracts with General Motors. We are glad for him, even though we suspect he is not really telling the country about the "or what" he knows too well. It *is* a great country for most Americans. But for an increasing number, the "or what" has become more a genuine question than a rhetorical statement. It is something like the emotions of a John Singleton finishing up a film in Simi Valley as the King trial was ending and the verdict was being handed down. Singleton, one of the bright new directors, seems poised to benefit from all that America promises: young, black, talented, movin' on up to the front seat of a Cadillac. But he knows, as does Trevino, that the "or what" of the question is the dark side of the "great country." Depending on where you stand, L.A. is the dark side of Simi Valley, or Simi Valley is the dark side of L.A.

When he asked, "Why can't we get along?" I assume Rodney King had black and white people in mind. It was white cops who beat him, and white cops get their mandate from a majority of white people. I imagine that a look inside King's head would reveal all sorts of white people running around as if in some slow-motion dream, ever-recurring, maddening, the kind that leaves one sitting up in bed screaming in the darkness. Getting along can be stated in a way that makes it sound so simple. Rodney King's personal story reveals that it is in fact complicated, that the complex problems and issues related to black-white tensions are not black and white.

Why can't Rodney and others like him get along? On the one hand, he was and is, quite obviously, not a saint. And white people are not responsible for his lifestyle, at least not entirely. Regardless of their circumstances, all people, including black people, have the capacity to make good choices instead of bad ones, to choose right over wrong.

On the other hand, it is inevitable that people—young or old, black or white—will make better choices when more of those better choices are available to them. When someone has a chance to net a couple of thousand dollars a week selling drugs, it is hard to make the right choice to work at McDonald's for minimum wage. It would be easier to choose to work in an air-conditioned office with an established, secure company at forty thousand dollars a year, plus benefits.

In this context, black people have always known that getting along in America is in some measure dependent upon

finding the favor of white people. In the small community of
black people where I grew up, people knew this, though they
rarely spoke about it. I never did hear anyone use the term
racist or *racism*. I can recall only one mention of discrimination
by my mother, and that was in a conversation about why she
did not attend church. Apparently she had felt the sting of
discrimination in one of the churches while she was a young
woman. Although she was a talented person, the accompanist
for the high school orchestra and many on-campus events, she
could not crack the exclusive, all-white enclave of one of the
town's fine congregations. She did not dwell on it, but it had a
profound affect on her.

Far to the south of my town, another black man was
experiencing a similar orientation to the vagaries of growing up
black in white America. Actor James Earl Jones was reared on
farms in Mississippi and Michigan by his grandparents—hard-
working farmers with values like those shared by their equally
hardworking white neighbors. He sucked in wisdom from both
sides of his family. By the time he was fourteen, he says, he
knew what outrage over racism was about:

> It colors your future. Your horizons have suddenly become
> quite limited and you don't quite understand why. I had two
> grandparents—one from whom I heard no rancor or racially
> motivated anything, and the other, all racially motivated. So I got
> doses of both realities and they are two separate realities. One is a
> world potentially free of the insanity of racism and one is riddled
> with the insanity of racism (James Ammeson, *Traveler*, North-
> west Airlines magazine, July 1992, pp. 42–43).

As there are at least two sides to most stories, so there are
different responses to the reality of racism.

Most of the young black people who were my contempo-
raries left small towns from Mississippi to Michigan upon
graduation from high school, if in fact they graduated. A good
part of the reason we left was that we had come to know that
those who defined "getting along" had excluded us from the
process. In our communities we saw no one of color working at
any respectable level in the work force. All the black men in
town pushed mops or served as domestics. Of course, some of

us learned that mops can be pushed with style, but we would not allow that to set the limits of our aspirations.

Sam Fullwood III had a similar experience. He recounts growing up outside of Charlotte, North Carolina, his eyes filled with stars, his ears vibrating with the sounds of marching feet and civil rights rhetoric. Of his upbringing amid segregation in the South, he says,

> My parents were born in rural North Carolina . . . never questioned the inequities of a segregated South . . . they sheltered us from the lingering traces of Jim Crow and imbued in us a belief that the evils of the outside world—I never heard the word racism in our household—could be made to disappear. If we worked hard, nothing was impossible (Interview, *Los Angeles Times Magazine*, 3 November 1991, p. 24).

Yet this representative of middle-class America, a successful journalist, admits to being more angry about America and its experience today than at any time in his life. He feels betrayed. Many of us know that feeling well. By all the standards set by his parents and his society, Fullwood has made it: a fine wife, three children, money to send them to good schools, a safe and comfortable place to live. So it is unsettling and profoundly significant to hear him say, "My generation—called the 'new black middle class' by one sociologist—is so disillusioned by the persistent racism that continues to define and limit us that we are abandoning efforts to assimilate into the mainstream of society. I see no end to this trend" (Ibid., p. 23).

The significance of Fullwood's confession is fairly clear, especially if he speaks for America's black middle-class professionals: If his achievements and commitments to the values of good ole Protestant America do not shield him from the debilitating effects of racism, how does the lower class find the answers to King's question?

Again, this does not seem to be a culture issue. Most of black middle-class America has paid its dues to Euro-American culture. What Fullwood and others are saying is that they have tried it and found it wanting. The problem is not ideology in the classic sense. There are numerous values to be derived from all that good Enlightenment stuff. The problem is that too many white people cannot or will not transcend their own system, or, put another way, cannot wrap flesh around the words they profess.

I suspect that we as a race are experiencing what Claude Steele calls "stigma, the endemic devaluation many blacks face in our society." We have come to realize that our presence in the broader society has very little influence on how that society views us. The same experience is shared by most black evangelicals.

This is why we rarely get invited to participate when our white brothers hold their banner events. Typically, one of us will be there, the one who currently enjoys the favor of the ruling elite. Because evangelicals choose to deal with only one of us at a time, we are never adequately represented. This ensures that no boats will be rocked. Meanwhile, the brother who gets invited to participate will make no difference. He will not be taken seriously. His purpose is merely to help the host assembly feel good about itself and to make sure that any true journalists who should happen by will take note that the platform was integrated. A black man might carry a flag into the arena, perhaps lead the morning devotionals, or on rare occasions be asked to deliver the keynote address. But he will not be present in the air-conditioned suite on the top floor where policy is made and the future course is determined. The movers and shakers will, however, make sure to give their guest plenty of bumper stickers announcing, for example, that the world will indeed be reached by the year 2000.

The inability of white and black evangelicals to work as full partners is one reason there is a National Association of Evangelicals and a National Black Association of Evangelicals. Conversations between these groups have gone on—and off— for years. It would be interesting to trace the course of these talks, especially as white evangelicals gained more and more access to power in high places.

My experience is that black evangelicals have never been taken seriously by the larger group. The issue, once more, has not been culture or the delineation of homogeneous units in the interest of evangelism. Rather, the struggle has been over the willingness, or the lack thereof, to share influence and power— in a word, control. I suspect this is largely the case today, in spite of efforts in the past several years to discuss the areas that divide us.

Control was clearly the issue in Manila as the changing of the guard among the Lausanne Committee (USA) was being paraded in front of the Americans assembled. The new leaders were, unsurprisingly, all white males. Whatever else Lausanne has been, it has been a good ole boys club. Since then, the guard has changed again in North America. The baton did get passed, as Leighton Ford said it would be. And it got passed to an old friend and crony, just as *I* said it would be. (See "A New Generation of Olds," *World Vision Magazine*, December 1989–January 1990, pp. 28–29.)

This transition in leadership is being hailed by some as a signal that the movement in the United States is gaining some of the momentum being experienced among evangelicals in Europe. It is hard for many black evangelicals to believe that a leadership so uniformly lily-white can signal a "trend toward the rejuvenation" the movement claims. Americans can get away with such talk when they go to Europe. After all, they are going home. But it sounds more like idle talk in their own backyard. Too many people of color know too much about those who are talking and the track records they boast.

This is the true center of the pain. The problem per se is not that black and white Christians have been all that we could have been and should have been together. Nor is the problem that blacks have not known how to behave or to speak their protests in ways that could be heard. Some of us are fairly articulate, and some even speak softly. The fundamental problem is that white people who own the system did not allow our absence to bother them. It did not dawn on enough of them that the real issue was the integrity of the Gospel itself and, consequently, the integrity of our witness to the rest of the world, a world wherein the majority is blessedly nonwhite.

Certainly those of us who have been invited to the conferences and meetings have done our part by playing the game. We have gotten to be pretty good at it through the years. But some of us, as we get older, have had attacks of integrity. Some might say we have become arrogant. In any case, today most black evangelicals—and more than a few white ones— view North American evangelicalism as a movement whose time has come and gone. This is a time in which, one would think, that sector of evangelicalism would want to open new rounds of discussion with their black and brown brothers.

"Can we get along?" I hear Rodney King's words through an experience nearly twenty-three years old. I was invited to deliver a keynote address at a luncheon of evangelicals in Kansas City. The occasion was the annual meeting of this national group. Arrayed on that dais were some of the legends of modern evangelicalism. I was impressed, of course. As I recall, the theme had something to do with moving forward together into the seventies.

I think I "blew it." In my rather youthful naïveté—I was only forty years old then—I argued that going forward together would mean making fewer trips to Jerusalem for prophecy conferences and paying more attention to the struggles for justice at home. We had just emerged from the fires of the sixties, and I thought then that God had given us another opportunity at the outset of a new decade to plant our evangelical feet firmly in the "bloody face of history" and make a difference. Afterward, I was comforted by the late Joe Bayly and a few others who knew something of the ache I carried inside but had somehow failed to express very well.

Twenty-three years later, as I conclude this work, I realize that perhaps I have failed to say it well this time, too. But in the midst of all the misunderstandings, hurt feelings, negative attitudes, and fundamental injustice that encompass the issues I have presented, one thing is certain: The evangelical community before God has the constant opportunity to be born again, to get into shape, to become everything it should and can be. Riots have a way of revolutionizing attitudes and assumptions, of confronting us with the reality we have been ignoring. The reality of a nation in danger of losing its moral and ethical moorings ought to awaken us. Urban centers throbbing with broken men and women ought to get our attention. A nation in danger of copping out on democracy ought to summon us all to reconsider the contributions we can make and to examine the degree to which we have sold out to the culture.

How can we, as an evangelical community, respond to this new era of challenges?

For starters, priorities need to change. We will need to

focus more on home base, even as we attempt to extend our ministries abroad. That focus must be on our cities. For those of us who live in America and its cities, it is not reassuring that, for instance, the Lausanne Committee International is excited about new ministries in Eastern Europe. The future agenda of this group reads like the reshaping of the European community. All of it comes under the masthead of "Building Bridges in a Divided World." This is a useful slogan—one that is, no doubt, right on target given the unleashing of all those ancient tribal brutalities in parts of the old continent. (We have learned that Europeans behave just like those uncivilized Africans just as soon as they are released from communist colonialism. The only difference is that their butchery is given a different cast in the popular and religious press. In Europe, this is a "struggle for democracy.")

American believers—many more than can be useful at this time—are heading for those parts in droves, bearing baggage of all sorts, often spreading among the brethren there the same sick sectarianism that has divided evangelicals at home. They go with gadgets and gimmicks and formulas galore. Someone ought to tell these brothers that if they don't address the plight of America and her cities, there might not be any place to land their jets upon their return home. America has become one of the toughest and neediest mission fields in the world. Democracy, so closely linked in the minds of many evangelicals with the Gospel itself, may triumph in Hungary while it slips through our fingers in our cities.

The effort to reorient ministries to North America and the city will not be easy. For one thing, it is much easier to raise money for Azerbaijan than for Oakland; Shaqlawah than South Bend. South Philadelphia makes a poor slide show compared with Sarajevo. American young people, able to raise necessary funds, are much more likely to end up in Bosnia than South Boston—much to the relief of their parents. Anglos feel more at ease in Hong Kong or Singapore than they do in America's inner cities. It is strange to realize how difficult it is to be white in one's own country, how much more comfortable it is for some to be among people of color faraway. Actually, it is tragic.

Money aside, it is difficult to think of America as a mission field. That is because there are so many churches here and the influence of Christianity has been so pervasive throughout our history. That influence is still very much alive, and there is still much saltiness in its functioning. America still makes no sense apart from its Judeo-Christian heritage. The churches of this country have been in the forefront of mission studies and mission giving. Evangelicals have led the world as a sending church, supplying a majority of the world's missionaries for decades, along with untold millions of dollars in support monies. The United States has been a gigantic launching pad from which Gospel rockets have been propelled to nations worldwide. Today, however, the launching pad has some cracks in it. The soil in which it is planted has begun to erode. The supplier is today desperately in need, and that need is not contained in the city.

The evangelistic challenge facing evangelicals in North America is posed largely by a culture that is thoroughly secular in nature and in spirit. It is difficult to imagine a more thorough, top-to-bottom capitulation to secularism by any society in the West than our own. Despite a semblance of Christian faith throughout the country and the seemingly robust growth of churches in some sectors of the country, the society has not surrendered its commitment to the basic premises supplied by the Enlightenment. We have finally progressed in our commitment to liberalism to the lofty pinnacles of modernity, and even the churches—especially the liberal branches—have basked in this bright light. The light is dimming. As "Dandy Don" Meredith used to say, "The party is over." And bells cast in a thousand places to celebrate freedom now have cracks in them, just like the one in Philadelphia.

George Bush would have given us a new world order and thousands of points of light. But his assumptions were grounded in the same old ideologies that have moved us closer to Armageddon. His crusade for values, and the values he has identified, sounded as if they came right out of a Protestantism that once defined this country and its values. But the fervency is gone. Today these words sound like hollow political catch-words, slogans for sound-bite commercials in the service of the party. They sounded like this for many of us because we know the words are separated from their root. They have no substance in a perspective and power dictated by the God of the ancient Scriptures. The talk about values is not grounded in truth and moral virtue.

It is this rootlessness of American cultural values that dooms any serious plans for a revitalization of the society based upon so-called values. This is especially true of economic solutions predicated on ideologies related to capitalism. This absence of moral and ethical values is, in Daniel Bell's phrase, "the cultural contradiction of capitalism."

Second, if the cities in the United States are to be served well, the church here must be revived. We are in desperate need of an outbreak of holiness and discipline in our congregations. That revival must in turn launch a more radical and aggressive era of evangelism, waged across a broad front. This new era must not be defined or controlled by the same people who have hoarded the enterprise for the past thirty years. New arenas range from inner-city neighborhoods to the universities. The simplistic formulas of the past will not be sufficient. We will need new training sessions to equip new evangelists to challenge the intellectual baggage of secularism in a time when it is apparent that the basic presuppositions of that secularism have lost much of their appeal.

These new evangelists must be composed of laity. The evangelical movement must launch an all-out attempt to equip all of God's people for ministry. So far, only feeble attempts at this have been registered. There are only a few prophets among us calling us to this work, only a few at the leading seminaries—which, unfortunately, is not surprising.

One aspect of a revived Protestantism would be a renewed commitment to lay ministry in the churches. The absence of trained laity has in many ways marginalized Christianity itself. It has contributed to the impression in the world and in the church that only professionals with impressive degrees can communicate good news. Preachers spend an inordinate amount of time urging followers to go into the world. The truth is, the church is already in the world from nine to five every day and most of the night. An enormous Christian presence is already situated where the world hurts. The problem is, it does not always know what to do there. It is often ill-equipped intellectually to understand the world of ideas that affect the way people behave and make choices. Lay people often have little idea how the current bankruptcy of ideas leaves the culture vulnerable to various ideologies and strange cultic notions about how humankind is to achieve the new world order. People are adrift, looking for answers; left unattended, they will find new and more exotic gurus to help them gain stability and meaning. They are also vulnerable to the Gospel for all the same reasons.

I thought of this as I drove out Century Boulevard to the Los Angeles airport not long ago. I read the billboards during this short, twenty-minute drive after exiting from the Harbor Freeway. Any stranger to Los Angeles could exegete a stretch between South Figueroa to Crenshaw Boulevard by reading the billboards and noting what products are being pushed, what people are being targeted. Camels smoke cigarettes here, and handsome black people can be seen smiling down at passers-by, assuring them that exotic booze guarantees success. (Such billboards can't be found in Beverly Hills or Bel Air or San Marino.) This is another kind of pollution, a kind that politicians and their well-off constituents are not interested in cleaning up. It is crass racism, aimed at making money off black and Latino people. When they are through here, they will take their scam to colored peoples abroad.

What really caught my eye during this trip, however, was a sign trumpeting another product: oneness. The overall caption reads "One," and the subtitles are "One God, One World, One Human Race, One L.A." I couldn't read the name of the sponsor, but I doubt that it was the Mayor's Task Force to Rebuild L.A. It had the sound and feel of the New Age movement. Certainly it portrayed the same, mystical, lofty ambitions characteristic of that movement. But I like the sentiment. To this point, attempts to respond to the challenges posed by varieties of New Age practice are concentrated in the suburbs. That is no surprise, since the movement itself is middle- to upper-middle class, sponsored by Americans who have time and money to invest in "finding themselves." The New Agers are deep into the suburbs, and they clearly intend to be players in the game of giving direction to the country. How does the church meet the challenge posed by this new form of an ancient heresy—especially since it makes no room for Jesus in its understanding of God?

Meanwhile, back downtown, other, less esoteric questions assert themselves. How will the African-American church equip its workers to take on the threat of the Nation of Islam? What about youth gangs? Who will assist churches in the Latino and black communities as they attempt to mediate between laborers scrambling for the few jobs available? How does the church in the black community deal with the threat of AIDS beyond a condom give-away after services on Sunday? How does it instill its traditional values about sex and family at a time when most babies are born to single women, many of them in their early teens?

Evangelical leaders face yet another threat to their ability to reorder priorities posed by what I call the "political correctness syndrome" (PCS). This virus has all but destroyed discussion of key social and moral issues in universities and colleges, seminaries, and the business place. Church pews are divided on many of the same issues as the rest of society: abortion, homosexuality, lesbianism, AIDS, and so on. This might be regarded as a healthy sign of a still lively intellectuality among us. Still, the best debates on these issues are probably heard in places where blue-collar workers gather on lunch break. These workers don't have development officers reading their latest publications or nervous constituents voting their pocketbooks when an outbreak of conviction seizes their leadership.

The virus has apparently affected evangelical churches, as evidenced by the widespread fuzziness surrounding conduct that ought to draw clear biblical condemnation. Euphemism is not very common in Scripture. David did not "sleep" with Bathsheba, as her pregnancy attested. Adultery and fornication, according to the Scriptures, are just that. And God displayed his faithfulness to David by sending Nathan to indict his heart on this matter. Where are the Nathans of our time?

Consider also the ethics of greed. Much quick money was made during the Reagan years by many conservative Christians. A lot of it found its way into missions' coffers and building plans for mega-churches. "Smart business practices" is a poor euphemism for greed. Where are our Nathans calling the church to repent over its sell-out to the god Mammon?

At risk in this morally uncertain atmosphere is the abandonment of any concept of church discipline on the one hand and a surrender of basic theological understandings of the nature of God on the other. It is not easy to discipline a member in many churches today for fear that the outraged saint will get a lawyer and sue. At best, the offended persons simply pack up and move elsewhere. At worst, a lawsuit costs the congregation a lot of money and a damaged reputation.

There are some congregations in urban America whose musical and preaching traditions are in the hands of gay and lesbian performers. Even though the theology that prevails among most in those pews is conservative—and in some cases focuses on deliverance from "the power of sin" as the chief motif—nothing is being said about the matter. The silence that obtains reflects the sentiment "live and let live." In the black church, this silence is understood in terms of a social ethic that is reluctant to expose, let alone expel, one of its own, no matter how aberrant the behavior. Discipline gives way to other values.

Another way to look at it is simply that we prefer a Savior who loves everybody, who refuses to call people sinners (which he didn't, incidentally), and who generally believes that how people behave is a private affair. Perhaps we are tired of a deity who is "of purer eyes than to behold iniquity" because we have become convinced that such a God is no more able to define iniquity than we are. After all, wouldn't anyone really prefer a God whose nature is love rather than One who is a "consuming fire"? In regard to morality and ethics, one is left to wonder whether the contemporary church is much different from those Americans outside its walls. I suspect the differences are not as great as we would like to think.

When it comes to analysis of the general moral decline of our culture and the need for the church to address that decline, agreement among black and white evangelical leaders is widespread. But there comes a point at which theological agreement breaks down. White scholars and church leaders seem to get uptight when nonwhites press the claim for a theology that liberates in the socio-political arena, even when that theology is offered, not as a replacement, but as an addendum to the personal-ethic agenda. There is concern also when a black scholar argues that African people can be found on the pages of the Old and New Testaments and that for this reason theology could not possibly be complete unless an African perspective be honored.

Why do people get upset when questions are raised about the rightness of whiteness ideology when applied to theology? If Euro-Americans can be charged with cultural chauvinism in the teaching of the so-called classics, why not when the same set of presuppositions prevails in theological discourse? If white seminaries do not loosen their ideological strings in these matters, they will become even less relevant for nonwhites than most of them are already.

In considering the overall mission and goals of the church, it seems to me there are three areas where it must reapply its special talents and insights. One is in the arena of ideas, and here it seems clear we must spend a good deal of time exploring the meaning of the biblical concept of reconciliation. Second, we must be more clear about the meaning of spirituality. We must search for its true meaning and application in the arena of social transformation. Finally, assuming we get to action, we must explore all the avenues open to us for cooperation and partnerships across our metropolitan communities.

In spite of all the carnage of the riots in Los Angeles, especially the horrors of needless death, these were not race riots. The country has not had one of those in many years. Even the riots in Detroit were not about "race," even though the *New Columbia Encyclopedia* refers to the event as "race riots in Detroit" (p. 753). That was in 1967, and that town has had enough experience with the real thing to know the difference. This is not to gloss over the intense, race-related animosity that still exists among Americans, nor the insidious racism that haunts white America, whether or not it is acknowledged. But there were no marauding white people roaming the streets of Los Angeles looking for black people to shoot. There were no black people driving through Simi Valley with shotguns poking out of the side windows. And there were plenty of instances in the heat of the battles when blacks came to the aid of whites— and vice versa.

The fact is that most Americans are people of good will. Most of us really do like other people, even those who are not like us. We prefer that they not be too close, however. We like those people in the abstract, not in the concrete. That is how black people view Koreans; how Koreans view Latinos; how Latinos view Anglos; and on and on. Yet, in spite of this peculiar sociology, many Americans will admit to having a friend who is "one of them." Usually we explain, "But he's different." At least it is a beginning. It is a good first step to have friends from these odd tribes, friends whom we often love and admire, who are concrete, who have names. More and more they are ending up as relatives.

There exists a fundamental contradiction between an American system that cherishes equity and the painful alienation experienced by many American citizens. That is why the theme of reconciliation has become a dominant one in our time. When alienation is for many a common reality, and animosity between people grows out of unrelieved pain, reconciliation is the only way to peace. This challenge could result in the finest hour for the church. Reconciliation is a biblical word. It is *our* word, and its ministry *our* enterprise. "God has given unto us the ministry of reconciliation." Truly, that should be at the core of our curriculum.

Unfortunately, reconciliation is no more a part of the church's experience today than it was in Corinth. And if we are called to proclaim reconciliation to the world, we ourselves must be "reconciled to God." How can the church in the African-American community become reconciled to the church in Koreatown? This is a crucial test, since these two communities have experienced the most painful and damaging encounters. How does the church in the black community view the encroachment of Latino peoples and their churches in territories long associated with being black in L.A.? Will their ministers and leaders make the necessary commitment to talk and pray together? The same questions apply to relationships between Japanese and Chinese congregations, Korean and Latino congregations, to all Christians across the ethnic spectrum. They also apply to relations between Protestant and Jewish congregations, especially black leaders and Jewish leaders.

Blacks and Jews have been allies for many years.* This has

*Black soldiers of the 761st Tank Battalion liberated the death camps at Dachau and Buchenwald. The 761st was an all-black unit that included a young been especially true since black people began moving from the rural South to the country's urban centers. Jews are an urban people. They understand what it takes to survive in urban contexts, especially urban ghettos. Without Jewish support, Tom Bradley could not have become the first black mayor of Los Angeles, nor would he have survived for nineteen years without their continued involvement.

But cities are changing. Relationships that were black and white, Jewish and black, are now more diverse. Latinos now vie for power in L.A. politics, and the next mayor may well be neither Hispanic or black. Michael Woo is running a strong challenge to all comers, and if he is successful, he will be the city's first Asian-American mayor. All this change has put enormous pressure on the Jewish leadership to chart a new course in urban politics. One thing is clear, however: The future of the Jewish community is urban, and this is true whether Jews are Orthodox, Reformed, liberal, or whatever.

But Jews are re-evaluating their relationship to the city and especially to the African-American community. These relations have been severely strained since the riots of the sixties and more recently since the politics of the Jimmy Carter and Jesse Jackson eras. Jews have been stung by the assault on their properties during urban riots, stung also by the vituperative remarks of Louis Farrakhan and the perception that black leaders have not distanced themselves from Farrakhan's rhetoric. This re-evaluation continues in spite of the sustained efforts of rabbis, political leaders, and such civic organizations as the Anti-Defamation League and the American Jewish Congress.

It is not easy for Jews to remain in the city. I watched the Jewish community abandon Detroit after that city's riots in the sixties. It was painful to see, even though I benefited from their exodus. I bought a fine house from a Jewish family. Since those years, occasioned by more urban unrest, crime, and worsening economic and educational prospects, Jews have been moving to the suburbs. They seem to have moved politically also—more and more to the right. The Jewish community in urban America

---

officer named Jackie Robinson. (See "Liberators," a PBS documentary, on this history.)

sees itself at the crossroads. The road they take will have a profound impact on the cities throughout the nation.

The basis for reconciliation between the Jews and other urban tribes is already present in the Jewish experience of oppression and in their long if tortuous relationship with the God who delivers and heals. It is resident in the concept of *shalom* and is related to the equally powerful quest for peace and transformation in the term *tikkun*. Of course, Christian understandings of the call to reconciliation, along with everything else in evangelical theology, is grounded in the Jewish Scriptures. Thus the groundwork for reconciliation has been laid out for centuries. What is needed today—more than ever—is the willingness of Protestants, Catholics, and Jews in urban America to accelerate the conversations of recent years and tie them to new activities to reinforce a flagging and fraying central city coalition.

The issue is not how Christian congregations might cooperate in an evangelistic strategy or church-growth crusade. Rather, the issue is whether disparate congregations of believers can network their faith in such a way as to demonstrate to a skeptical society that believing in Jesus as Lord makes a difference in human relations. One might make a strong argument for a moratorium on church growth. Who needs more segregated churches when a whole city is up for grabs?

I am aware of how heretical this sounds, and I am of course aware of the biblical mandate to spread the Gospel to all the world. I have also heard some leaders argue that God must not have intended the church to promote reconciliation between races, given that there are so few examples of it around. (The observation, at least, is accurate.) From there one could argue that the reason for this condition is that God respects these enclaves of ethnicity so much that he is reluctant to tamper with them lest they be diverted from planting other churches among their own kind. So each group continues on its own, simply preaching the Gospel, building churches here and there, and hoping that in the process of perfecting they will find each other.

The bottom line is that the church is still the most segregated community in America. We have not found each other, except on the annual rent-a-choir day. So a moratorium on church growth for the purpose of majoring in reconciliation might not be such a bad idea. The witness it would show to a confused society grappling for ways to mend broken fences could just result in the greatest growth the church has witnessed in quite a while.

The impression I get from my colleagues in psychology, pastoral care, and counseling is that reconciliation is hard work. It requires confrontation, getting beyond mere words to true feelings and attitudes, many of which we may not even be aware. Of course, this presumes we must be in the same room together. Beyond that, it requires setting up listening posts where we can speak with one another about the things that have kept us apart. The church ought to be such a listening post. This must become the preoccupation of the church's leadership. Unless it does, the church will be mute before the ravages of on-going racial and ethnic animosity.

I believe that the future of human relations in our cities is ultimately in the hands of churches. It is here where politicians, cops, citizen-victims of police brutality, business leaders, moms and pops from those small stores—all sorts of people—could meet to talk, perchance to pray. Some fine ministry work is already being done among urban gangs, but gang members are regarded as the scum of the earth by too many people in too many churches. We need to view these wandering youths as "sheep . . . scattered . . . without a shepherd." Who will mediate between these gang members and the local police precinct? Probably not the police chaplain—he is too much of a cop himself or he wouldn't be accepted by the establishment. The answer might emerge if community-based policing becomes fully operative. Then cops might get names, and gang members faces. But until that happens, and even after it does, the church has an important role to play.

If the churches are to play out this key role in reconciling alienated persons and groups, the church must be present. In fact, if churches are to contribute to peace and reconciliation, they must plant deeper roots in the communities where their buildings stand. There are too many fine congregations whose leadership is not connected to the community, whose Reverend has not ventured out into the neighborhood for years, anymore than most of his flock. They are not in touch with the people in the community as they once were when the members lived nearby. The neighbors look on and wonder what sacrifices are made behind those stained-glass windows on Sunday. The church no longer "exegetes" the neighborhood. Instead, the neighborhood exegetes the church's parking lot and finds it empty, except on Sunday mornings.

This reflects long-known research that the old neighborhood church is a thing of the past. This is even true of many former Roman Catholic "parish" churches. The old parish is gone. Indeed, in most urban settings, neighborliness is something of a rarity—yet it is a deeply desired experience. In many places, community must be rebuilt, and this again is a Judeo-Christian concern. Most ethnic groups with roots in non-European cultures look upon community as the fundamental unit of human life. The churches must build on this tradition.

If we move from a discussion of reconciliation to spirituality, we move a short distance. New Testament writers regularly make the connection, as Paul did when writing to the fractious community at Corinth. The apostle John makes a similar case in his letters, albeit in different words. Check out Moses and the prophets and you will find they all say the same thing: Professions to know God are empty if justice and mercy do not obtain between people. The point stressed by these writers is that spirituality is the shortest distance between two people. Reconciliation is at heart a matter of spirituality.

Spirituality is also the wellspring for evangelistic effort and for social activism. Gustavo Gutierrez, known mostly for his work in liberation theology, confessed this in his book on spirituality. He called it, "We Drink From Our Own Wells." Evangelicals have for years been trying to get evangelism and social responsibility together. Major conferences have been held on evangelism, most of them haunted by the ministry and words of Martin Luther King, Jr., and the equally powerful voices from the non-West—Orlando Costas, for example, arguing for an integrated approach to the church's total task. But the debate has been between those committed to evangelism and those committed to justice. What we should be striving for is a spirituality that will inform both evangelism and social transformation. Jesus evangelized out of who he was. He was Good News; therefore he proclaimed good news. He came to express the heartbeat of his Father, and out of that consuming passion and a heart of obedience he preached and taught and healed among the distressed.

We must discover a biblical spirituality that serves as a basis for all our activity as Christians, including reconciliation. In this regard, we ought to explore the significance of the Holiness movement in our own country in order to find connections between a passion to spread scriptural holiness across the land and the reformation of the nation. Anyone working in theology at Drew University would recognize that as the flaming ambition of early Methodists. Timothy Smith long ago demonstrated that early evangelicals did not choose between revivalism on the one hand and social reform on the other. They did both, the latter out of the experience of the former. Early Pentecostals, before they started becoming mainline evangelicals and card-carrying conservatives, had some powerful breakthroughs in reconciliation among black and white believers. Their theology was about ethics in human relations. We need to open ourselves to this history and to this experience of the holy.

Whatever spirituality is—and there is no one definition to satisfy us all—it is more than a personal experience. If it is the life of God within, it ought to address the way we live our lives publicly. That view is confirmed by Jesus' life. In him, Life spoke to life; Life called forth life.

For some, spirituality is about signs and wonders and casting out evil spirits. There is a place for that, of course, as Jesus demonstrated. And if it deserves a more prominent place than most of us grant it, let us find some exorcists and go after the powers that be across a broad cultural front, including politics and economics.

I recall a student relating to the class how a certain evangelist, before beginning a crusade in a city, arrives early, gets a room in a hotel, and fasts and prays, wrestling with the demons that control the city. I asked the student, "Which demons does he take on?" I sensed he didn't quite get my meaning, so I asked, "Did he take on the demons of capitalism and industry, or did he confine himself to those denizens of the darkness who ply their trade up and down Sunset Boulevard?" The exchange opened up some interesting dynamics.

I rather suspect that the spirituality we need inclines more toward the development of character and the discovery of our own deep needs in community with those who are often at our mercy. If I am right, then spirituality must move, change directions, find new partners. It will move from city to suburb, from suburb to city, from South to North and back again. The burden will always be upon the hearts of those of us who prosper while professing spirituality. We have benefited most from the resources and jobs and advantages the society offers. We knew how to ask the right questions of the right people at the right time. We are the ones who often claim that it was God who led us, supplied our needs. If so, then the burden is ours to translate the benefits of this spiritual edge so that reconciliation happens in concrete ways, ways through which God's concern for all his children is demonstrated.

Finally, a word about action. Any religious experience that authentically knows God finally translates into action in God's behalf. I have grown wary of the word *action*, as, for instance, in "social action." The term is as redundant as "social Gospel." What other kind of Gospel is there? What kind of action is there that is not social, that does not at some level involve people? Americans are an action-oriented people. Watch the movies and you will see white folks saving the world, with an occasional dark face thrown in for political correctness. Read the ads in *Christianity Today* and *Moody Monthly* and you will find a plethora of institutions, institutes, and seminars with high-energy believers promising to equip their own kind for action. But rarely does one find even a hint that this action is aimed at our urban crises. No doubt, a lot of good things happen at these events, things that enable suburban churches to feel good about themselves. These gatherings are also good for book and cassette sales. When I attend these events, I have a chance to renew some old friendships but find very little I care to take home.

So while these conferences convene at plush hotels, others will work on getting their act together in the city. The resources there are incredibly rich—culturally, spiritually, even financially in some quarters. We may decide, after some really hard work and painful dealing with the alienation that separates us, that we can bring peace and reconciliation to the city without outside help. I suspect it would be a relief to many suburban churches to know they are not really needed in the city. It would make the barbecue taste even better.

But for other suburban churches, the future demands a fresh look at ways they can be reconnected with brothers and sisters downtown. A recent conversation with the Reverend Eddie Edwards on Detroit's East Side confirms that partnerships between believers and people of good will are proving more than adequate in breaking down old animosities and developing old neighborhoods.* Other examples are to be found in most of our metropolitan areas from Pasadena to Peoria. So despite what must sound to some like cynicism, I want to be an idealist.

In the sixties, a black activist claimed that black people needed white people to be free from their fear, and white people needed black people to be free of their guilt. Some of that is still true, but I suspect fear and guilt no longer constitute the prevailing emotional ethos. Black people and white people still view each other warily and from a distance. Other ethnic groups have been sucked into the vortex of the storm, and all of us for sometime to come will be struggling to get past the tempation to avoid caring about each other one way or the other. Neither fear nor guilt is the issue. The issue, twenty-seven years after Watts, is love. But then, that is asking for a whole lot.

---

*Edwards's work, called Joy of Jesus, is one of the finest examples of community development I have yet seen.